Creative Keto Kitchen

Copyright © 2019 Miyuki Minami
All rights reserved
No part of this publication should be reproduced or distributed in any form or by any means, electrical or mechanical or stored in a database without prior permission from the publisher.

ISBN: 978-1-075109-83-6
Published Independently

The author (Miyuki Minami aka 'Keto Diet Channel') is not a licensed practitioner, physician, or medical professional. The information presented herein is not intended to diagnose, treat, cure, or prevent any disease. Full medical clearance from a licensed physician should be obtained before beginning or modifying any diet, exercise, or lifestyle program, and physicians should be informed of all nutritional changes. The author claims no responsibility to any person or entity for any liability, loss, or damage caused or alleged to be caused directly or indirectly as a result of the use, application, or interpretation of the information presented herein.

* Stevia Powder and Liquid Stevia used in these recipes are a SweetLeaf® brand:
  - SweetLeaf® Stevia Sweetener Shaker
  - SweetLeaf® Sweet Drops™ Liquid Stevia
  If you'd like to use other sweeteners, follow the conversion calculator below:
  https://sweetleaf.com/stevia-conversion-calculator/
You can enter the amount specified in these recipes in the second one 'Amount of Stevia Powder', and then use the amount shown in 'Amount of Sugar'. However, there's no guarantee that the texture of yours will be same as mine.

Introduction

I'm Miyuki Minami, a self-taught home cook. Because I'm Japanese and English is my second language, I may need to ask you to excuse my English from time to time.

I used to be a vegan for about nine years from 2007 through December 2015, and turned directly to low carb eating in January 2016. Finding vegan products or vegan-friendly restaurants, or simple healthy natural products in Japan is very difficult, so I always needed to cook for myself when I was on the vegan diet. Even on the low carb ketogenic diet now, it's still sometimes difficult to find good restaurants or cafes, or products at grocery stores. Japan is a country which is filled with products made with sugar, MSG, and artificial ingredients. If you want to take good care of yourself here in Japan, I believe that cooking for yourself is a must. I was kind of forced to cook for myself when I adopted the vegan lifestyle, but I have been enjoying cooking very much since then.

So, one year after I turned to the low carb ketogenic diet, I decided to share my recipes with those on the same diet as me in other countries through the recipe blog called 'Keto Diet Channel'. I ran this blog for two and a half years. Although I have more recipe ideas in my mind and more and more people are following my Facebook page and Pinterest, I decided to shut down my blog due to some reasons... (I'm still on keto, though.) However, I wanted to keep all my recipes in some way because I devoted so much of my time, money, energy, and effort to create them. I did everything on my own with no help from others, from developing recipes to shooting and editing photos and videos to writing posts on my blog. So, now I'm self-publishing this cookbook which contains all those recipes plus three new easy ones. (I apologize if there are any typos!)

Some of my recipes, such as Babka, Tiramisu, Lingots au Chocolat, and Ice Cream Tacos, became very popular on Facebook and Pinterest. Also, as most of my recipes are creative and unique, you may recognize some of them from the pictures in this cookbook if you are on Facebook or Pinterest.

I hope you enjoy my low carb ketogenic recipes as much as I enjoyed developing them!

* All of my recipe videos except for three recipes newly created for this cookbook can still be found on the following sites:

www.youtube.com/ketodietchannel

www.facebook.com/ketodietchannel

Creative Keto Kitchen

CONTENTS

Muffins & Donuts	4
Cookies	10
Cakes	14
Pies & Tarts	58
Frozen Treats	71
More Treats	82
Drinks	97
Pastries & Bread	99
Main Dishes	136
Soups	158
Appetizers & Snacks	166
Recipe Index	186

VANILLA CUSTARD BLUEBERRY MUFFINS

Prep Time 15 minutes
Cook Time 30 minutes
Total Time 45 minutes
+ Chilling Time
Servings 8 muffins

Ingredients

Vanilla Custard Cream
- 3 Egg Yolks
- 1 tbsp Stevia Powder
- 3/4 cup (180 cc) Heavy Cream
- 1/4 tsp Xanthan Gum
- 1 to 3 tsp Vanilla Extract (Adjust to your liking)

Muffin Batter
- 1.76 oz (50 g) Almond Flour (1/2 cup: Measure by weight if possible)
- 1 oz (28 g) Coconut Flour (1/4 cup: Measure by weight if possible)
- 1 tbsp (or less) Stevia Powder
- 1 tsp Aluminum-Free Baking Powder
- 3 Eggs
- 1 oz (28 g) Coconut Oil, Melted
- 1/4 cup (60 cc) Heavy Cream
- 2 tbsp Lemon Juice
- 1/2 cup (70 g) Blueberries (Frozen or Fresh)

Instructions

Vanilla Custard Cream
1. Whisk the egg yolks and stevia powder in a bowl until pale yellow.
2. Add the xanthan gum. Mix well.
3. Bring the heavy cream to almost a simmer in a saucepan. Add to the egg yolk mixture. QUICKLY whisk to combine, and then transfer the mixture to the saucepan.
4. Keep stirring the mixture with a spatula over low - medium heat. DON'T STOP!

5. When it starts to thicken, stir 20 - 30 more seconds. (* It takes 3 - 4 minutes to thicken.)
6. Turn off the heat and stir 20 - 30 more seconds. Add the vanilla extract and mix well.
7. Strain the custard cream through a fine mesh sieve to make it smooth. Pour the custard into a tray and level out.
8. Place a piece of cling wrap over the custard. Stick the wrap to the custard by pressing lightly to prevent a film from forming on top of the custard.
9. Refrigerate for one hour or until cold.
10. Remove the custard from the fridge. Remove the wrap carefully and transfer the custard to a bowl.
11. Cream the custard with a whisk. (* Add a little bit of heavy cream if too thick to cream it.)
12. Optional: Place in a piping bag.
13. Refrigerate while preparing the muffin batter.

Muffin Batter
1. Preheat the oven to 180 C / 350 F. Grease your muffin tin very well or line with paper baking cups.
2. In a medium bowl, whisk together the dry ingredients.
3. In a large bowl, whisk well the eggs, coconut oil, heavy cream and lemon juice. Add the dry ingredients and mix well.

Assembly
1. Spoon 1/2 of the batter evenly into each muffin cup. Pipe (or spoon) 1/2 of the custard evenly on top of each (but do not pipe or spoon all the way to the edge). Then, sprinkle 1/2 of the blueberries on top. Repeat with the remaining batter, custard and blueberries. (* You'll have 6 layers: batter -> custard -> blueberries -> batter -> custard -> blueberries.)
2. Bake for 20 - 25 minutes.
3. Let cool on a wire rack.

Recipe Notes:
Keep refrigerated. Bring to room temperature before serving.

Approximate Nutritional Values Per Serving:
Calories 279 kcal, Protein 6.4 g, Total Fat 25.6 g, Total Carbohydrate 5.7 g, Dietary Fiber 2.3 g, Sugar 2.3 g

CREAMY LEMON CURD RASPBERRY MUFFINS

Prep Time 10 minutes
Cook Time 23 minutes
Total Time 33 minutes
+ Chilling Time
Servings 8 muffins

Ingredients

Lemon Curd
- 2 Large Eggs
- 2 Large Egg Yolks
- 1/2 cup (120 cc) Lemon Juice
- 2 tsp Stevia Powder
- 1/4 tsp Xanthan Gum
- 2 oz (56 g) Unsalted Butter

Muffin Batter
- 1.76 oz (50 g) Almond Flour (1/2 cup: Measure by weight if possible)
- 1 oz (28 g) Coconut Flour (1/4 cup: Measure by weight if possible)
- 1 tbsp Stevia Powder
- 1 tsp Aluminum-Free Baking Powder
- 2 Large Eggs
- 2 Large Egg Whites
- 3 tbsp (45 cc) Heavy Cream
- 2 oz (56 g) Raspberries, Roughly Chopped (Frozen / Fresh)

Instructions

Lemon Curd
1. Whisk the eggs, egg yolks and lemon juice in a saucepan.
2. Add the stevia and xanthan gum and whisk well to combine.
3. Add the butter and cook the mixture over low - medium heat, stirring / whisking vigorously until thick. Remove from the heat.
4. Strain the lemon curd through a fine mesh sieve into a bowl.

5. Place a piece of cling wrap over the curd. Stick the wrap to the curd by pressing lightly.
6. Chill for one hour or until cold.

Muffin Batter
1. Preheat the oven to 180 C / 350 F. Grease your muffin tin well or line with paper baking cups.
2. In a medium bowl, whisk together the almond flour, coconut flour, stevia and baking powder.
3. In a large bowl, whisk well the eggs, egg whites and heavy cream. Add the dry ingredients and whisk well to combine.
4. Add 1/2 cup (120 g) of the lemon curd and stir well to combine. (* Reserve the rest of the lemon curd for later. Also, if using fresh raspberries, you can fold 1/2 of them into the batter here.)

Assembly
1. Spoon 1/2 of the batter evenly into each muffin cup. Sprinkle 1/2 of the raspberries evenly on top of each. Then spoon the remaining batter over the raspberries.
2. Bake for 7 minutes.
3. (Work fast.) Remove the muffin tin from the oven. Spoon the remaining lemon curd on top of the muffins. Then sprinkle the remaining raspberries.

4. Bake for another 10 - 12 minutes.
5. Let cool on a wire rack.

6. Remove the muffins very carefully from the tin because the lemon curd on top is very creamy.

Recipe Notes:
Keep refrigerated. Bring to room temperature before serving.

Approximate Nutritional Values Per Serving:
Calories 192 kcal, Protein 7.1 g, Total Fat 15.9 g, Total Carbohydrate 5.8 g, Dietary Fiber 2.3 g, Sugar 2.4 g

TWO-TONE CINNAMON DONUTS

Prep Time 10 minutes
Cook Time 15 minutes
Total Time 25 minutes
Servings 6

Ingredients

Batter
- 3 oz (85 g) Almond Flour
- 2 tbsp Coconut Flour
- 1 tsp Ground Cinnamon
- 1/2 tsp Aluminum-Free Baking Powder
- 1/8 tsp Xanthan Gum
- 1 tbsp Stevia Powder
- 3 Large Eggs
- 5 tbsp Melted Coconut Oil (Measure melted)
- 1 tsp Vanilla Extract

Cinnamon Mix
- 1.5 tbsp Ground Cinnamon
- 1/2 tsp Stevia Powder

Cream Cheese Frosting
- 4 oz (112 g) Cream Cheese, Softened
- 1 oz (28 g) Coconut Oil or Unsalted Butter
- 1/4 cup (60 cc) Heavy Cream
- 1 tbsp Stevia Powder
- 1 tsp Vanilla Extract

Instructions

Batter
1. Preheat the oven to 180 C / 350 F. Grease each cavity of your donut pan very well if not silicone. (* A silicone mold is highly recommended.)
2. In a medium bowl, whisk together the almond flour, coconut flour, cinnamon, baking powder, xanthan gum and stevia.
3. Add the eggs, coconut oil and vanilla to a food processor and blend well.
4. Add the dry ingredients to the food processor and blend until well-combined.
5. Divide the batter into 2 equal portions. Add the cinnamon mix ingredients into one of them and mix well.
6. Place each portion of the batter into a separate piping bag, and pipe alternately into each cavity of the donut pan.

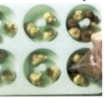

7. Flatten out the batter by dropping the pan several times or using a spoon.
8. Bake for 12 - 15 minutes.
9. Let cool for about 15 minutes and then remove from the pan.

Cream Cheese Frosting
1. Process all the ingredients in a food processor / blender until smooth and creamy.

Approximate Nutritional Values Per Serving
Sans Frosting**:**
Calories 261 kcal, Protein 7.6 g, Total Fat 23.5 g, Total Carbohydrate 6.6 g, Dietary Fiber 3.8 g, Sugar 1.0 g

COCONUT COOKIES

Prep Time 10 minutes
Cook Time 15 minutes
Total Time 25 minutes
Servings 15 cookies

Ingredients

- 1.5 oz (45 g) Coconut Flour (1/3 cup: Measure by weight if possible)
- 1/3 cup (35 g) Unsweetened Shredded Coconut
- 1 tbsp Stevia Powder
- 1/2 tsp Aluminum-Free Baking Powder
- A Pinch of Sea Salt
- 2.5 oz (70 g) Coconut Oil, Melted
- 1 Large Egg
- 1 tsp Vanilla Extract

Instructions

1. Preheat the oven to 180 C / 350 F.
2. Add all the dry ingredients to a large bowl and whisk well.
3. Add the wet ingredients to the dry ingredients and mix well.
4. Roll the dough into 1-inch / 2.5 cm balls and place on a baking sheet lined with parchment paper. Smash down with a fork in one direction, and then the opposite direction.
5. Bake for about 15 minutes, or until really golden brown.
6. Allow to cool for 5 minutes on the baking sheet, and then transfer to a wire rack to cool completely.

Recipe Notes:
Bake your cookies really well until golden brown for a toasted coconut flavor.
Store them in the freezer for a hard texture. These cookies are soft at room temperature.
Approximate Nutritional Values Per Serving:
Calories 67 kcal, Protein 1.1g, Total Fat 6.0g, Total Carbohydrate 2.3 g, Dietary Fiber 1.5 g, Sugar 0.3 g

CINNAMON CHOCOLATE COCONUT FLOUR COOKIES

Prep Time 7 minutes
Cook Time 17 minutes
Total Time 24 minutes
Servings 14 cookies

Ingredients
- 4 tbsp (30 g) Coconut Flour
- 3 tbsp Unsweetened Cocoa Powder
- 1 tbsp Ground Cinnamon
- 1 tsp Aluminum-Free Baking Powder
- 1 tbsp Stevia Powder
- A Pinch of Sea Salt
- 2 Large Eggs
- 2.5 oz (70 g) Coconut Oil, Melted
- 1 tsp Vanilla Extract
- 1 tbsp Unsweetened Shredded Coconut for Topping (Optional)

Instructions
1. Preheat the oven to 180 C / 350 F.
2. In a medium bowl, whisk together the dry ingredients.
3. Add the wet ingredients and mix well. Let sit for a couple of minutes.
4. Drop one tablespoon of dough per cookie on a baking sheet lined with parchment paper. (* Arrange them into a round shape with your hands if desired.)
5. Optional: Sprinkle the shredded coconut on top.
6. Bake for 13 - 15 minutes
7. Allow to cool for 5 minutes on the baking sheet, and then transfer to a wire rack to cool completely.

Recipe Notes:
Store them in the freezer (or the fridge) for a hard texture. These cookies are very soft (almost cake like) at room temperature.
Coconut four varies greatly between brands. If you feel your cookies are dry, add more coconut oil next time.

Approximate Nutritional Values Per Serving:
Calories 72 kcal, Protein 1.6 g, Total Fat 6.5 g, Total Carbohydrate 2.5 g, Dietary Fiber 1.2 g, Sugar 0.9 g

LEMON CREAM CHEESE COOKIES

Prep Time 10 minutes
Cook Time 40 minutes
Total Time 50 minutes
Servings 14 cookies

Ingredients

- 2 Lemons (Remove wax with vegetable brush)
- 3.5 oz (100 g) Almond Flour (1 cup: Measure by weight if possible)
- 1 tbsp Stevia Powder
- 1/2 tsp Aluminum-Free Baking Powder
- 1.5 oz (42 g) Unsalted Butter, Softened
- 1 oz (28 g) Cream Cheese, Softened
- 1 Egg
- 1 tsp Vanilla Extract
- Powdered Sweetener (Optional)

Instructions

1. Preheat the oven to 110 C / 230 F.
2. Trim the ends of one of the lemons and slice thinly into 14 slices. (* See the Recipe Notes below.)
3. Place the lemon slices on a baking sheet lined with parchment paper.
4. Bake for 20 minutes.
5. Let cool.
6. Zest the other lemon. (* Should yield about one tablespoon. Use all of it later.) Then, cut it in half and juice. (* Use only one tablespoon later.)
7. Preheat the oven to 160 C / 320 F.
8. Whisk together the almond flower, stevia, and baking powder in a bowl.
9. In another bowl, beat the cream cheese and butter. Add the egg, vanilla, lemon zest, and one tablespoon lemon juice. Beat to combine.
10. Beat in the almond flour mixture until well combined.
11. Use a cookie scoop to scoop 14 balls of the dough onto the baking sheet lined with parchment paper.
12. Place one baked lemon slice on top of each ball and press very very lightly. (* Do not flatten because they will flatten while baking.)

13. Bake for 16 - 20 minutes, until the edges are lightly golden.
14. Allow to cool for 5 minutes on the baking sheet, and then transfer to a wire rack to cool completely.
15. Optional: Dust with the powdered sweetener.

Recipe Notes:
Keep refrigerated in an air tight container or a ziploc bag.
They freeze well. Defrost in the fridge for a few hours.
If you are not a fan of the bitter taste of cooked lemons, simply omit the slices (but doing so will make your cookies look very simple), or you can remove pith and rind as much as you can. If you leave the rind like the pictures, slice your lemon very very thinly (about 0.04 inch (1 mm) thick). If the rind is too thick, they will taste a bit bitter as described above and it'll also be hard to bite off.

Approximate Nutritional Values Per Serving:
Calories 84 kcal, Protein 2.4 g, Total Fat 7.6 g, Total Carbohydrate 2.6 g, Dietary Fiber 1.1 g, Sugar 0.9 g

LINGOTS AU CHOCOLAT

Prep Time 10 minutes
Cook Time 20 minutes
Total Time 30 minutes
+ Chilling Time
Servings 12 slices

Ingredients

Brownie Base
- 2 oz (56 g) Unsweetened Baking Chocolate, Chopped
- 1/2 cup (120 cc) Heavy Cream
- 1.76 oz (50 g) Almond Flour (1/2 cup: Measure by weight if possible)
- 2 tbsp Unsweetened Cocoa Powder
- 2 tsp Stevia Powder
- A Pinch of Sea Salt
- 2 Large Eggs
- 2 tsp Vanilla Extract

Chocolate
- 1 1/3 cups (320 cc) Heavy Cream
- 5 oz (140 g) Unsalted Butter, Cubed
- 7 oz (200 g) Unsweetened Baking Chocolate, Finely Chopped
- 1 tbsp Liquid Stevia
- 2 tsp Vanilla Extract
- 2 tbsp Rum (Omit if you want to go completely sugar free. Also, you can sub red wine)

Topping
- 1 tsp Unsweetened Cocoa Powder

Instructions

Brownie Base
1. Preheat the oven to 190 C / 375 F. Fold parchment paper to the size of the top of your loaf pan. (* An 8.5 x 3.6 inch / 22 x 9 cm pan was used for the cake in the pictures. An 8 x 4 inch / 20 x 10 cm pan also works, but the cake will be much flatter.)
2. Bring the heavy cream to a simmer in a saucepan over low heat. Turn off the heat. Add the unsweetened chocolate. Stir until melted and smooth. Set aside.
3. In a large bowl, whisk well the almond flour, cocoa powder, stevia powder and salt. Add the chocolate mixture and mix well. Then, add the eggs and vanilla and mix well.
4. Place the folded parchment paper in a dish / pan that is a bit bigger than the folded lines. Pour the brownie mixture within the folded lines and level out. (* It's okay to go over the folded lines.)

5. Bake for 13 - 15 minutes.
6. Remove from the oven and let cool completely. (* Preferably refrigerate for a few hours after reaching the room temp for it to be hard so that it will be easier to handle later.)
7. When cooled, cut off the edges so that it will fit into the top of the loaf pan.

Chocolate
1. Bring the heavy cream to a simmer in a saucepan over low heat and then add the butter. Turn off the heat when the butter is half melted.
2. Add the unsweetened chocolate and liquid stevia. Leave a couple of minutes. Then, stir slowly until melted and smooth.

3. Add the vanilla and rum and mix.
4. Pour the chocolate mixture into the prepared loaf pan lined with parchment paper. Smooth the surface.
5. Refrigerate for about 10 - 20 minutes, or until when the surface starts to solidify.
6. Remove from the fridge and place the brownie base onto the chocolate. Attach well.
7. Chill overnight.

To Serve
1. Remove from the fridge. Invert on a cutting board and then carefully remove the parchment paper.
2. Dust with the cocoa powder.
3. To slice, let sit out at room temperature for about 30 minutes (or less when the room temp is hot) before slicing. Heat a knife under hot water and wipe off the excess water before each slice.
4. To serve, after removing your slices from the fridge, let sit out at room temperature for 10 - 30 minutes (depending on the room temp and your liking).

Recipe Notes:
Keep refrigerated.
Approximate Nutritional Values Per Serving:
Calories 403 kcal, Protein 5.4 g, Total Fat 40.8 g, Total Carbohydrate 9.4 g, Dietary Fiber 4.1 g, Sugar 1.6 g

ALMOND BUTTER BROWNIES

Prep Time 5 minutes
Cook Time 25 minutes
Total Time 30 minutes
Servings 12 pieces

Ingredients
- 1 cup (240 g) Unsalted Almond Butter
- 1 Large Egg
- 1 tbsp Stevia Powder
- 1 tbsp Cocoa Powder
- 1/2 tsp Aluminum-Free Baking Powder
- 1 tsp Vanilla Extract
- 3 tbsp Water (or Almond Milk)
- 1/2 cup (70 g) Sugar Free Chocolate Chips

Instructions
1. Preheat the oven to 180 C / 350 F.
2. Add all the ingredients except for the chocolate chips to a food processor / blender and blend until smooth.
3. Fold in the chocolate chips.
4. Pour the batter into an 8 x 8 inch / 20 x 20 cm pan (or a smaller pan) lined with parchment paper.
5. Bake for 17 - 22 minutes.
6. Let cool for 15 minutes.

Approximate Nutritional Values Per Serving:
Calories 140 kcal, Protein 5.2 g, Total Fat 12.2 g, Total Carbohydrate 8.1 g, Dietary Fiber 3.8 g, Sugar 0.8 g

CARAMEL SWIRL POUND CAKE

Prep Time 20 minutes
Cook Time 1 hour
Total Time 1 hour 20 minutes
Servings 10 slices

Ingredients

Caramel Sauce
- 1.5 tbsp (20 g) Unsalted Butter
- 1/3 cup (45 g) Confectioners Swerve
- 1/2 cup (120 cc) Heavy Cream
- 1/8 tsp Xanthan Gum

Pound Cake
- 1.76 oz (50 g) Almond Flour (1/2 cup: Measure by weight if possible)
- 2 tbsp Coconut Flour
- 1 tbsp Whey Protein Powder
- 1 tsp Aluminum-Free Baking Powder
- 1/2 tsp Ground Cinnamon
- 1/2 cup (112 g) Unsalted Butter, Softened
- 2 tsp Stevia Powder
- 3 Medium to Large Eggs, Beaten (Room Temp)
- 1 tsp Vanilla Extract

Toppings
- Remaining Caramel Sauce
- 1 tsp Heavy Cream (Adjust) (Optional)
- 0.5 oz (14 g) Chopped Walnuts

Instructions

Caramel Sauce
1. In a saucepan over medium - low heat, combine the butter and Swerve. Bring to a boil, stir occasionally as needed and cook until browned (about 3 minutes). Turn off the heat.
2. Add one tablespoon of the heavy cream. The mixture will rapidly bubble. When it ceases, add the remaining heavy cream. Stir over medium - low heat until it thickens.
3. Turn off the heat and sprinkle with the xanthan gum. Whisk well to combine.

4. Turn on the heat again and stir over medium - low heat for about 20 - 30 seconds or until it gets thicker.
5. Set aside.

Pound Cake
1. Preheat the oven to 180 C / 350 F. Line an 8 x 4 inch / 20 cm x 10 cm loaf pan with parchment paper. (* The pan used for the cake in the pictures is 8.5 x 3.6 inch / 22 x 9 cm.)
2. In a medium bowl, whisk well the almond flour, coconut flour, whey protein powder, baking powder and cinnamon. Set aside.
3. In a large bowl, beat the butter about one minute at high speed. Add the stevia and beat about 2 minutes at high speed.
4. Beat in the eggs in 5 additions, scraping down the sides of the bowl as necessary. Add the vanilla in the last addition. (* Make sure to beat well between each addition (for about a minute).)
5. Add the dry and stir well.
6. Transfer 1/3 of the batter (or a bit less than that) to a separate bowl. Add 1/3 cup (80 g) caramel sauce to that bowl and stir well. (* The caramel sauce should crystalize by this stage, so stir over low heat until creamy before adding.)
7. Add about one teaspoon of the caramel sauce to the remaining plain batter and stir well.
8. Pour the caramel batter into the plain batter bowl and stir lightly (only 4 - 5 times) to create swirls.
9. Pour the batter into a pan. Drop the pan a few times to level out.
10. Bake for 45 - 50 minutes. (* Cover with aluminum foil halfway through the baking.)
11. Let cool in the pan for 15 minutes. Then remove from the pan and cool with parchment paper on.

Toppings
1. Stir the remaining caramel sauce over low heat until creamy. (* Add the heavy cream if too thick.) Place in a piping bag and pipe over the cooled cake.
2. Sprinkle the chopped walnuts.

Approximate Nutritional Values Per Serving:
Calories 233 kcal, Protein 4.3 g, Total Fat 22.7 g, Total Carbohydrate 3.0 g, Dietary Fiber 1.4 g, Sugar 0.8 g
(Swerve is not counted as carbs as it doesn't affect blood sugar levels.)

CHOCOLATE & CARAMEL MOUSSE CAKE WITH COFFEE CARAMEL GLAZE

Prep Time 20 minutes
Cook Time 18 minutes
Total Time 38 minutes
+ Chilling Time
Servings 8 slices

Ingredients

Sponge
- 1.76 oz (50 g) Almond Flour (1/2 cup: Measure by weight if possible)
- 1 tsp Stevia Powder
- 1/2 tsp Ground Cinnamon
- 1/4 tsp Aluminum-Free Baking Powder
- 1 Egg
- 1 oz (28 g) Unsalted Butter, Melted
- 1 tsp Vanilla Extract

Caramel Mousse
- 1.5 tbsp (20 g) Unsalted Butter
- 1/3 cup (45 g) Confectioners Swerve
- 1/2 cup (120 cc) Heavy Cream
- 1/8 tsp Xanthan Gum
- 1.5 tbsp Water
- 1.5 tsp Gelatin
- 1.5 tbsp Boiling Water
- 1/3 cup (80 cc) Heavy Cream
- A Pinch of Sea Salt

Chocolate Mousse
- 1.5 tbsp Water
- 1.5 tsp Gelatin
- 2 tbsp Boiling Water
- 3/4 cup (180 cc) Heavy Cream
- 4.5 tbsp Unsweetened Cocoa Powder
- 3/4 tbsp Stevia Powder
- 1 tsp Vanilla Extract

Coffee Caramel Glaze
- Remaining Caramel Sauce
- 2 tsp Strong Coffee

Instructions

Sponge
1. Preheat the oven to 180 C / 350 F. Fold parchment paper to the size of the top (opening) of your loaf pan. Then fold again, sharing one of the longer lines (= 2 rectangles). (* An 8.5 x 3.6 inch / 22 x 9 cm pan is used for the cake in the pictures. An 8 x 4 inch / 20 x 10 cm pan also works but the cake will be much flatter.)

2. In a bowl, whisk well the almond flour, stevia powder, cinnamon and baking powder.
3. In a different bowl, beat the egg for 2 minutes at high speed. Add the butter and vanilla and beat another minute. Then, add the dry and stir well.
4. Place the folded parchment paper on a baking sheet. Pour the batter within the folded lines and level out.

5. Bake for about 10 minutes.
6. Remove from the oven. Carefully invert on a cooling rack. Remove the parchment paper very carefully and let cool completely.
7. When cooled, place a cutting board over the sponge and then invert. Carefully remove the cooling rack because the sponge may be sticking to the rack. Then cut the sponge to the size of the top and the bottom of your loaf pan.

8. Line the loaf pan with parchment paper and place the bottom sponge, with the baked side facing up. Set aside.
(* Carefully wrap the other sponge in parchment paper and then in plastic wrap because the sponge may stick to the plastic wrap without parchment paper.)

Caramel Mousse
1. In a saucepan over medium - low heat, combine the butter and Swerve. Bring to a boil, stir occasionally as needed and cook until browned (about 3 - 5 minutes). Turn off the heat.
2. Add one tablespoon of the heavy cream. The mixture will rapidly bubble. When it ceases, add the remaining heavy cream. Stir over medium - low heat until it thickens.
3. Turn off the heat and sprinkle with the xanthan gum. Whisk well to combine.
4. Turn on the heat again and stir over medium - low heat for about 20 - 30 seconds or until it gets thicker.
5. Let cool to body temperature.
6. In a bowl, beat the heavy cream and salt until stiff peaks form.
7. In a small bowl, soften the gelatin by soaking in the water for a couple of minutes. Add the boiling water and stir to dissolve the gelatin. Set aside.
8. Add 1/3 cup (80 g) of the caramel sauce to the whipped cream (* Reserve the remaining caramel sauce for the glaze) and stir with a spatula. Add the gelatin mixture and stir.

9. Pour over the bottom sponge in the loaf pan.
10. Refrigerate for 2 hours.

Chocolate Mousse
1. In a small bowl, soften the gelatin by soaking in the water for a couple of minutes. Add the boiling water and stir to dissolve the gelatin. Set aside.
2. In a separate large bowl, beat the rest of the ingredients until hard.
3. Add the gelatin mixture and beat until combined.
4. Remove the loaf pan from the fridge and spread the chocolate mousse over the caramel mousse.
5. Place the other remaining sponge onto the chocolate mousse, with the baked side facing down.
6. Refrigerate for 2 hours or until set.

Coffee Caramel Glaze
1. Reheat the remaining caramel sauce until creamy if necessary. Add the coffee and mix well.
2. Remove the loaf pan from the fridge. Invert onto a plate or a cutting board. Carefully remove the parchment paper.
3. Spread the glaze on top.

Approximate Nutritional Values Per Serving:
Calories 310 kcal, Protein 4.2 g, Total Fat 38.7 g, Total Carbohydrate 4.4 g, Dietary Fiber 1.5 g, Sugar 2.2 g
(Swerve is not counted as carbs as it doesn't affect blood sugar levels.)

TIRAMISU

Prep Time 20 minutes
Cook Time 15 minutes
Total Time 35 minutes
+ Chilling Time
Servings 12 - 16

Ingredients

Cookies
- 7 oz (200 g) Almond Flour (2 cups: Measure by weight if possible)
- 2 tbsp Coconut Flour
- 2 tsp Stevia Powder
- 1/2 tsp Ground Cinnamon
- 1/4 tsp Salt
- 4 oz (112 g) Unsalted Butter, Melted
- 1 tsp Vanilla Extract

Filling
- 1 cup (240 cc) Heavy Cream
- 2 tbsp Stevia Powder
- 8 oz (227 g) Cream Cheese, Room Temp
- 10 oz (280 g) Mascarpone Cheese, Room Temp
- 2 tsp Vanilla Extract

Coffee Syrup
- 1/2 cup (120 cc) Strong Coffee, Room Temp
- 2 tbsp Rum (Omit if you want to go completely sugar free)
- 1 tsp Liquid Stevia

Topping
- 1 to 2 tbsp Unsweetened Cocoa Powder

Instructions

Cookies
1. Cut parchment paper into a rectangle a little bigger than 16 x 8 inch / 40 x 20 cm. Fold it to make 2 8-inch / 20 cm squares. (* This is because an 8-inch square baking dish is used to build up the tiramisu in the pictures. Change the size according to your dish.)

2. Preheat the oven to 180 C / 350 F.
3. Combine all the ingredients in a bowl. Mix well until a soft dough forms.
4. Place the dough within the folded lines of the parchment paper. Evenly press within the rectangle.

5. Cut the dough into half along the folded line of parchment paper. Then cut each square into 12 pieces.

6. Bake for 15 - 20 minutes. (* See the Recipe Notes below.)
7. Let cool completely. (* They are a bit brittle and hard to handle when warm.)

Filling
1. In a large bowl, beat the heavy cream and stevia until stiff peaks form.
2. In a separate bowl, cream the cream cheese. Add the mascarpone and stir well to combine. Add the vanilla and stir well.
3. Fold in the whipped heavy cream into the cream cheese mixture in 2 - 3 parts.

Coffee Syrup
1. In a small bowl, mix well the coffee, rum and liquid stevia.

Assembly
1. Arrange 1/2 (12 pieces) of the cookies into the bottom of an 8-inch / 20 cm square dish. Spoon 1/2 of the coffee syrup all over them. Then, spread 1/2 of the filling over the cookies into an even layer. (* Optional: If you want to decorate the top later, reserve some of the filling mixture before spreading it.)
2. Arrange the remaining cookies over the filling and spoon the remaining coffee syrup over them. Spread the remaining filling over the cookies into an even layer.
3. Optional: Place the reserved filling mixture into a piping bag and pipe over the tiramisu as you like.
4. Generously dust with cocoa powder.
5. Cover with plastic wrap and chill for 6 hours (or preferably overnight).

Recipe Notes:
Bake the cookies for about 20 minutes for a harder texture (easier to handle). In that case, let the tiramisu sit overnight for the cookies to get completely moist. If the baking time is 15 minutes (although ovens vary), the cookies might be brittle, which requires less time in the fridge to get moist. Either way, let the cookies cool completely before building up.

Approximate Nutritional Values Per Serving:
- 1/16:
  Calories 336 kcal, Protein 5.9 g, Total Fat 32.3 g, Total Carbohydrate 5.0 g, Dietary Fiber 1.9 g, Sugar 1.9 g
- 1/12:
  Calories 448 kcal, Protein 7.9 g, Total Fat 43.0 g, Total Carbohydrate 6.7 g, Dietary Fiber 2.6 g, Sugar 2.6 g

NO-BAKE PEANUT BUTTER CHOCOLATE ZEBRA CHEESECAKE

Prep Time 14 minutes
Cook Time 1 minute
Total Time 15 minutes
+ Chilling Time
Servings 6 - 8 slices

Ingredients

Base
- 2.64 oz (75 g) Almond Flour (3/4 cup: Measure by weight if possible)
- 1.5 tbsp Unsweetened Cocoa Powder
- 1/2 tsp Stevia Powder
- A Pinch of Sea Salt
- 1 oz (28 g) Unsalted Butter, Melted
- 1/2 tsp Vanilla Extract

Chocolate Mixture
- 1.5 oz (42 g) Unsweetened Baking Chocolate, Chopped
- 1/4 cup (60 cc) Heavy Cream
- 1/2 tsp Liquid Stevia
- 1 tbsp Vanilla Extract

Peanut Butter Cheesecake
- 1/3 cup (100 g) Unsweetened Peanut Butter, Room Temp
- 7 oz (200 g) Cream Cheese, Room Temp
- 1/2 cup (120 cc) Heavy Cream
- 2 tsp Vanilla Extract
- 2 to 3 tsp Stevia Powder

Instructions

Base
1. Line the bottom of a 6-inch / 15 cm removable bottom round cake pan with parchment paper. (* You can line the sides too for easier removal.)
2. In a mixing bowl, whisk the almond flour, cocoa, stevia and salt.

3. Add the butter and vanilla. Stir until a soft dough forms.
4. Spread the dough into the prepared pan.
5. Set aside.

Chocolate Mixture
1. Bring the heavy cream to a simmer over low heat. Remove from the heat.
2. Add the unsweetened chocolate. Stir until melted and smooth.
3. Add the stevia and vanilla and mix well.
4. Set aside.

Peanut Butter Cheesecake
1. In a large bowl, beat the cream cheese with an electric mixer until smooth. Add the peanut butter and beat until combined.
2. In another bowl, beat the heavy cream, stevia powder and vanilla until soft peaks form.
3. Add the whipped cream to the cream cheese mixture. Beat until combined.
4. Transfer about 1/3 of the batter to a separate bowl and add the chocolate mixture to that bowl. Beat until combined and smooth.
5. Transfer 1.5 tbsp of the white batter to the center of the chocolate base and then 1.5 tbsp of the chocolate batter to the middle of the white batter. Repeat with the remaining batters until all the batter is gone, giving the pan a shake to level the batter off every now and then.

6. Take a toothpick and drag lines outwards from the center to the edge of the cake.

7. Refrigerate overnight (or at least 4 hours).
8. Run a knife around the edge of the pan and remove the cake from the pan.

Approximate Nutritional Values Per Serving:
- 1/8:
Calories 373 kcal, Protein 8.0 g, Total Fat 36.1 g, Total Carbohydrate 7.7 g, Dietary Fiber 2.9 g, Sugar 2.2 g
- 1/6:
Calories 497 kcal, Protein 10.7 g, Total Fat 48.1 g, Total Carbohydrate 10.3 g, Dietary Fiber 3.8 g, Sugar 2.9 g

COCONUT FLOUR VANILLA LAYER CAKE WITH BLUEBERRY FILLING

Prep Time 15 minutes
Cook Time 25 minutes
Total Time 40 minutes
+ Chilling Time
Servings 6 slices

Ingredients

Cake
- 6 Eggs, Separated
- A Pinch of Sea Salt
- 1.23 oz (35 g) Coconut Flour (1/3 cup: Measure by weight if possible)
- 1 tbsp Stevia Powder
- 1 tsp Baking Powder
- 1/2 cup (120 cc) Heavy Cream
- 1.5 oz (42 g) Coconut Oil, Melted
- 2 tbsp Vanilla Extract

Frosting
- 1/3 cup (42 g) Frozen Blueberry, Thawed
- 1/2 tsp Lemon Juice
- 3 oz (85 g) Cream Cheese, Softened
- 3/4 cup (180 cc) Heavy Cream
- 1.5 tsp Stevia Powder
- 2 tsp Vanilla Extract

Toppings (Optional)
- Blueberries, Toasted Desiccated Coconut, etc

Instructions

Cake
1. Preheat the oven to 180 C / 350 F.
2. In a large bowl, beat the egg whites and salt until stiff peaks form.
3. In a small bowl, whisk well the coconut flour, stevia and baking powder.
4. In a separate bowl, whisk the egg yolks until a bit pale. Add the heavy cream, coconut oil and vanilla and mix well.

5. Add the dry ingredients to the yolk mixture and mix well. Let sit for a couple minutes. Then, fold the whites into the mixture in 3 parts.
6. Pour the batter into 2 different 6-inch / 15 cm round cake pans lined with parchment paper (or silicone pans).
7. Bake for 22 - 25 minutes. Let the cakes sit in the oven for another 10 minutes. (* The cakes puff up while baking, but sink while you are letting them sit in the oven.)
8. Let the cakes cool in the pans for about 10 minutes. Remove from the pans and let cool completely. Then cut each cake in half horizontally.

Frosting
1. In a food processor / blender, process the blueberries, lemon juice and one tablespoon of the cream cheese. Set aside.
2. In a large bowl, beat the heavy cream, stevia and vanilla until stiff peaks form. Add the remaining cream cheese and beat until combined. Add 1/4 of the mixture to the blueberry mixture and mix well.

Assembly
1. Spread 1/2 of the blueberry frosting evenly over one bottom layer, leaving 1/3-inch / 1 cm border. (* When spreading the blueberry frosting, do not spread all the way to the edge.) Top with the upper cake layer. Spread some of the cream cheese frosting evenly all the way to the edge. Top with the other bottom layer and spread the remaining blueberry frosting evenly, leaving 1/3-inch / 1 cm border. Top with the last cake layer and press very lightly.

2. Spread the remaining cream cheese frosting evenly over the top and sides of the cake.
3. Chill until set (preferably overnight).

Recipe Notes:
The cake gets moister and tastes better the day after.

Approximate Nutritional Values Per Serving
Sans Topping**:**
Calories 434 kcal, Protein 9.5 g, Total Fat 40.3 g, Total Carbohydrate 6.5 g, Dietary Fiber 2.4 g, Sugar 3.1 g

THREE LAYER RASPBERRY CHEESECAKE MOUSSE TERRINE

Prep Time 15 minutes
Cook Time 5 minutes
Total Time 20 minutes
+ Chilling Time
Servings 10 slices

Ingredients

Raspberry Puree
- 3 oz (85 g) Frozen Raspberries
- 1 tsp Lemon Juice
- 1/2 tsp Liquid Stevia

Cheesecake Mousse Terrine
- 8 oz (227 g) Cream Cheese, Softened
- 1 tbsp Stevia Powder
- 1 tbsp Lemon Juice
- 1 tsp Vanilla Extract
- 1 cup (240 cc) Heavy Cream
- 3 tbsp Warm Water
- 0.3 oz (9 g) Gelatin (About 1 tbsp)

Chocolate Glaze
- 0.5 oz (14 g) Coconut Oil
- 0.75 oz (21 g) Unsweetened Baking Chocolate, Chopped
- 3 tbsp Heavy Cream
- 1/2 tsp Liquid Stevia
- 1 tsp Vanilla Extract

Instructions

Raspberry Puree
1. Add the frozen raspberries, lemon juice and liquid stevia to a saucepan.
2. Stir well and crush them lightly as they begin to release their juice over low heat. Cook until you have a thick sauce.
3. Remove the saucepan from heat.
4. Strain the seeds out.
5. Let cool completely.

Cheesecake Mousse Terrine
1. In a large bowl, beat the heavy cream with a hand mixer until very thick. (* Stop beating right before soft peaks begin to form).
2. In another large bowl, cream the cream cheese using the same hand mixer. Add the stevia, lemon juice, vanilla and beat until smooth and well-combined.
3. In a small bowl, sprinkle the gelatin over warm water and stir to dissolve the gelatin. (* If your gelatin doesn't dissolve in warm water, dissolve in cold water first, soak for a couple minutes and then warm in a double boiler or a microwave.)
4. Add the gelatin mixture to the cream cheese mixture and beat to combine.
5. Fold in the whipped cream.
6. Divide the mixture into 3 equal portions.
7. Transfer one portion of the cream cheese mixture to a loaf pan lined with parchment paper. (* An 8.5 x 3.6 inch / 22 x 9 cm pan is used for the cake in the picture. An 8 x 4 inch / 20 x 10 cm pan also works, but the cake will be much flatter.) Level out and drop the pan a few times. Freeze for 5 minutes while working on the next step.
8. Add about 2 teaspoons (or about 1/3) of the raspberry puree to one of the remaining portions of the cream cheese mixture and stir to combine. (* Use a whisk if necessary.) Place over the bottom layer. Level out and drop the pan a few times. Freeze the pan for 5 minutes while working on the next step.

9. Add the remaining raspberry puree to the last portion of the cream cheese mixture and stir to combine. Place over the second layer. Level out and drop the pan a few times.
10. Chill overnight, or at least 4 hours until set.
11. Invert onto a plate or a cutting board. Remove from the pan and then remove the parchment paper carefully.
12. Pour the chocolate glaze on top and chill for 5 minutes, or until set.
13. To slice, heat a knife under hot water and wipe off the excess water before each slice.

Chocolate Glaze
1. Melt the coconut oil in a saucepan over low heat. Remove from the heat when half melted.
2. Add the unsweetened chocolate. Let stand for a couple minutes. Stir until melted and smooth.
3. Add the heavy cream, liquid stevia and vanilla and mix well.

Approximate Nutritional Values Per Serving:
Calories 207 kcal, Protein 3.6 g, Total Fat 20.5 g, Total Carbohydrate 3.1 g, Dietary Fiber 0.7 g, Sugar 2.0 g

TRICOLOUR BUNDT CAKE (VANILLA, CHOCOLATE & CINNAMON)

Prep Time 15 minutes
Cook Time 40 minutes
Total Time 55 minutes
Servings 10 - 12

Ingredients

Chocolate Mixture
- 1/4 cup (60 cc) Unsweetened Coconut Milk
- 1.5 oz (42 g) Unsweetened Baking Chocolate, Chopped
- 1/2 tsp Liquid Stevia
- 1/2 tsp Vanilla Extract

Cake
- 7 oz (200 g) Almond Flour (2 cups: Measure by weight if possible)
- 1.5 tbsp Coconut Flour
- 2 tbsp Stevia Powder
- 1.5 tsp Aluminum-Free Baking Powder
- 5 Large Eggs
- 1/3 cup (80 cc) Unsweetened Coconut Milk (See the Recipe Notes below)
- 1 oz (28 g) Coconut Oil, Melted
- 1 tbsp Vanilla Extract
- 2 tbsp Ground Cinnamon

Toppings (Optional)
- Powdered Sweetener, Whipped Cream, etc

Instructions

Chocolate Mixture
1. Bring the coconut milk to a simmer in a saucepan over low heat. Remove from the heat.

2. Add the unsweetened chocolate and let stand a couple minutes. Then, stir until melted and smooth.
3. Add the liquid stevia and vanilla and mix well. Set aside.

Cake
1. Preheat the oven to 170 C / 325 F.
2. In a medium bowl, whisk together the almond flour, coconut flour, stevia powder and baking powder.
3. In a large bowl, beat the eggs until pale and fluffy (2.5 - 3 minutes at high speed). Add the coconut milk, coconut oil and vanilla and mix well. Add the dry ingredients and mix well.
4. Transfer 1/4 of the batter to a separate bowl. Add the chocolate mixture to that bowl and mix well.
5. Divide the remaining batter into 2 equal portions and add the cinnamon to one of them and mix well. (* Now you have 3 colors of batter.)
6. Transfer the batter (about 2 - 3 tbsp each) alternately to a silicone 10-inch / 25 cm bundt pan. (* If not silicone, grease your pan well.) Slightly shake the bundt pan to even the batter.

7. Bake for 30 - 40 minutes.
8. Let cool on a wire rack.
9. Optional: Dust with powdered sweetener. Enjoy with whipped (coconut) cream.

Recipe Notes:
Coconut four varies greatly between brands. If you feel your cake is dry, please reduce the amount next time.
The thickness of coconut milk can also vary by brand. If your coconut milk is very thick, dilute with water and make it to 1/3 cup. The consistency should be like almond milk.

Approximate Nutritional Values Per Serving:
- **1/10:**
  Calories 247 kcal, Protein 9.0 g, Total Fat 21.5 g, Total Carbohydrate 8.8 g, Dietary Fiber 4.6 g, Sugar 1.4 g
- **1/12:**
  Calories 206 kcal, Protein 7.5 g, Total Fat 17.9 g, Total Carbohydrate 7.4 g, Dietary Fiber 3.8 g, Sugar 1.2 g

CARAMEL CHEESECAKE BARS

Prep Time 10 minutes
Cook Time 1 hour 12 minutes
Total Time 1 hours 22 minutes
+ **Chilling Time**
Servings 16 slices

Ingredients

Crust
- 5.3 oz (150 g) Almond Flour (1 1/2 cups: Measure by weight if possible)
- 1/4 cup (18 g) Unsweetened Cocoa Powder
- 1 tsp Stevia Powder
- 1/4 tsp Salt
- 2.25 oz (65 g) Unsalted Butter, Melted
- 1 tsp Vanilla Extract

Caramel Sauce
- 3 tbsp (1.5 oz / 42 g) Unsalted Butter
- 2/3 cup (90 g) Confectioners Swerve
- 1 cup (240 cc) Heavy Cream
- 1/4 tsp (or a bit less) Xanthan Gum

Caramel Cheesecake Layer
- 14 oz (400 g) Cream Cheese, Room Temp
- 1/2 tsp Stevia Powder
- 2 Eggs
- All of Caramel Sauce
- 2 tsp Unsweetened Cocoa Powder

Instructions

Crust
1. Preheat the oven to 180 C / 350 F.
2. In a mixing bowl, whisk well all the dry ingredients.
3. Add the butter and vanilla. Stir until dough comes together.

4. Press evenly onto the bottom of an 8 x 8 inch / 20 x 20 cm pan lined with parchment paper.
5. Bake for about 10 minutes.
6. Let cool.

Caramel Sauce
1. In a saucepan over medium - low heat, combine the butter and Swerve. Bring to a boil, stir occasionally as needed and cook until browned (about 3 - 5 minutes). Turn off the heat.
2. Add one tablespoon of the heavy cream. The mixture will rapidly bubble. When it ceases, add the remaining heavy cream. Stir over medium - low heat until it thickens.
3. Turn off the heat and sprinkle with the xanthan gum. Whisk well to combine.
4. Turn on the heat again and stir over medium - low heat for about 20 - 30 seconds or until it gets thicker.
5. Let cool until slightly warmer than body temperature.

Caramel Cheesecake Layer
1. Preheat the oven to 320 F / 160 C.
2. In a large bowl, cream the cream cheese and stevia with a hand mixer or whisk.
3. Add one egg at a time and mix well each time, scraping down the sides of the bowl if necessary.
4. Add the caramel sauce in 3 parts and mix well each time, scraping down the sides of the bowl if necessary.
5. Reserve about 3 tablespoons of the mixture. Pour the remaining mixture over the baked crust.
6. Add the cocoa powder to the reserved mixture and mix well. Place in a piping bag. Pipe in lines over the cheesecake mixture. Drag a skewer back and forth across the lines.

7. Bake for 50 - 55 mins.
8. Let cool completely in a pan on a wire rack. (* The cheesecake will jiggle in the center, but it will set as it cools.)
9. Once it's cool, cover and chill in the fridge overnight (or at least 4 hours). Do not remove the cheesecake from the pan yet.
10. Remove the cheesecake from the pan after the refrigeration.
11. Slice and enjoy.

Approximate Nutritional Values Per Serving:
Calories 273 kcal, Protein 5.6 g, Total Fat 26.5 g, Total Carbohydrate 3.9 g, Dietary Fiber 1.4 g, Sugar 1.7 g
(Swerve is not counted as carbs as it doesn't affect blood sugar levels.)

Creative Keto Kitchen

ZEBRA CAKE

Prep Time 20 minutes
Cook Time 30 minutes
Total Time 50 minutes
Servings 6

Ingredients

Chocolate Mixture
- 1.5 oz (42 g) Unsweetened Baking Chocolate, Chopped
- 1/4 cup (60 cc) Heavy Cream
- 1 tsp Liquid Stevia
- 1 tsp Vanilla Extract

Cake
- 3 oz (85 g) Almond Flour (3/4 cup: Measure by weight if possible)
- 1 tbsp Coconut Flour
- 1 tbsp Stevia Powder
- 1 tsp Aluminum-Free Baking Powder
- 3 Large Eggs
- 2 oz (56 g) Coconut Oil, Melted
- 1 tsp Vanilla Extract

Instructions

Chocolate Mixture
1. Bring the heavy cream to a simmer in a saucepan over low heat. Remove from the heat.
2. Add the unsweetened chocolate. Stir until melted and smooth.
3. Add the liquid stevia and vanilla and mix well. Set aside.

Cake
1. Preheat the oven to 180 C / 350 F.
2. In a medium bowl, mix together the almond flour, coconut flour, stevia and baking powder.
3. Add the eggs, coconut oil and vanilla to a food processor / blender and blend well.
4. Add the dry ingredients to the food processor and blend until uniform.
5. Transfer about 6 tablespoons of the batter to another bowl. Add the chocolate mixture to that bowl and mix well.
6. Transfer the batter (about 1.5 tablespoons each) alternately to the center of a 6-inch / 15 cm round cake pan lined with parchment paper.

7. Drop the cake pan a few times to get the air bubbles out.
8. Bake for 25 - 30 minutes.
9. Let cool on a wire rack for about 15 minutes.

Approximate Nutritional Values Per Serving:
Calories 299 kcal, Protein 7.8 g, Total Fat 28.4 g, Total Carbohydrate 7.0 g, Dietary Fiber 3.5 g, Sugar 1.1 g

CHOCOLATE TERRINE

Prep Time 20 minutes
Cook Time 16 minutes
Total Time 36 minutes
+ **Chilling Time**
Servings 12 slices

Ingredients

Chocolate Terrine
- 6.5 oz (185 g) Unsweetened Baking Chocolate, Finley Chopped
- 3/4 cup (180 cc) Heavy Cream (Must be warm around 105 F / 40 C)
- 1 tbsp + 2 tsp Stevia Powder (Adjust to your liking)
- 4 Eggs, Beaten
- 4 oz (112 g) Unsalted Butter, Melted (Must be warm around 105 F / 40 C)
- 2 tsp Vanilla Extract
- 1/3 tsp Unsweetened Cocoa Powder (To Dust)

Whipped Cream
- 3/4 cup (180 cc) Heavy Cream
- 1 to 2 tsp Stevia Powder (Adjust to your liking)
- 2 tsp Vanilla Extract

Instructions

Chocolate Terrine
1. Preheat the oven to 160 C / 320 F. Line a loaf pan with parchment paper. (* The pan used for the cake in the pictures is an 8.5 x 3.6 inch / 22 x 9 cm pan, but an 8 x 4 inch / 20 x 10 cm pan also works.)
2. Add the unsweetened chocolate and warm heavy cream to a double boiler and allow to melt (which takes about 10 minutes). Stir occasionally. (* Tips: Remove the double boiler from the heat once the temperature of the water in the bottom pot reached around 60 C / 140 F, place the bottom pot on a pot stand and work on the whole process, with the top bowl still placed on top of the bottom pot.)

3. At the same time, warm the eggs using another double boiler to around 85 F / 30 C. Then, sieve.
4. Add the stevia powder to the chocolate mixture and stir slowly until combined. (* The mixture may be gritty at this point.)
5. Add the warm eggs in 4 parts. Whisk well between each addition until well combined and glossy. (* Even if the mixture separates, keep going. It should come together in the end.)
6. Add the warm melted butter. Then add vanilla. Whisk well until well combined.
7. Pour the mixture into the pan and level out. Drop the pan a few times.
8. Set the loaf pan in a roasting pan. Pour hot water into the roasting pan to a depth of about 0.4 inch / 1 cm. (* You can use the hot water from the double boiler.)
9. Bake for 14 - 16 minutes. (* Do not over-bake.)
10. Remove the roasting pan from the oven. (* It's okay to remove even if the terrine still looks moist / jiggly in the middle.) Remove the loaf pan from the water bath and let cool to room temperature in the pan.
11. Cover the pan lightly and refrigerate overnight in the pan.
12. Remove from the fridge. Invert on a cutting board and remove the parchment paper.
13. Dust with the cocoa powder and let sit until the terrine reaches room temperature before slicing.
14. To slice, heat a knife under hot water and wipe off the excess water before each slice.
15. Keep refrigerated. To serve, let your slices sit at room temperature for 10 - 60 minutes (depending on the room temp and your liking). Or you can warm your slices in a toaster oven for a few minutes or microwave for 20 seconds and enjoy oozing molten centers. Serve with whipped cream.

Whipped Cream
1. Beat the heavy cream, stevia powder, and vanilla until stiff peaks form.

Recipe Notes:
Keep refrigerated. Eat within 7 days.
Please try to keep the temperature of the mixture at 30 C / 85 F to 40 C / 105 F while working.
Approximate Nutritional Values Per Serving:
- **With** Whipped Cream:
  Calories 280 kcal, Protein 4.5 g, Total Fat 29.0 g, Total Carbohydrate 5.9 g, Dietary Fiber 2.5 g, Sugar 1.0 g
- **Without** Whipped Cream:
  Calories 232 kcal, Protein 4.2 g, Total Fat 23.4 g, Total Carbohydrate 5.5 g, Dietary Fiber 2.5 g, Sugar 0.6 g

NO-BAKE CHEESECAKE WITH LEMON CURD FILLING

Prep Time 15 minutes
Cook Time 5 minutes
Total Time 20 minutes
+ Chilling Time
Servings 12 slices

Ingredients

Lemon Curd
- 2 Eggs
- 2 Egg Yolks
- 1/2 cup (120 cc) Lemon Juice
- 1 tbsp Stevia Powder
- 1/4 tsp Xanthan Gum
- 2 oz (56 g) Unsalted Butter

Base
- 1 1/2 cups Toasted Nuts (1 cup almonds, 1/4 cup walnuts and 1/4 cup pecan nuts are used for the cheesecake in the pictures)
- 2 oz (56 g) Unsalted Butter, Melted
- 1 tsp Stevia Powder

Cheesecake
- 1 1/2 cups (360 cc) Heavy Cream
- 13 oz (370 g) Cream Cheese, Room Temp
- 2 tbsp Stevia Powder
- 3 tbsp Lemon Juice
- 2 tsp Vanilla Extract
- 1 tbsp Grated Lemon Zest
- 1/3 cup (90 g) Sour Cream
- 2 tbsp Water
- 4 tsp Gelatin
- 1/4 cup (60 cc) Boiling Water

Instructions

Lemon Curd
1. Whisk together the eggs, egg yolks, lemon juice and stevia in a saucepan.
2. Add the xanthan gum and whisk well to combine.
3. Add the butter and cook the mixture over low - medium heat, stirring frequently until thick. Remove from the heat.
4. Strain the lemon curd through a fine mesh sieve into a bowl.
5. Place a piece of cling wrap over the curd. Stick the wrap to the curd by pressing lightly.
6. Chill for one hour or until cold.

Base
1. Add the toasted nuts to a food processor and pulse until finely ground.
2. Add the butter and stevia and blend well.
3. Press evenly into the bottom of an 8-inch / 20 cm springform pan.
4. Chill while preparing cheesecake.

Cheesecake
1. In a large bowl, beat the heavy cream until very thick with a hand mixer. (* Stop beating just before soft peaks begins to form.)
2. In a large bowl, cream the cream cheese using the same hand mixer. Add the stevia, lemon juice, vanilla, lemon zest and sour cream and beat until smooth and well-combined.
3. In a small bowl, soften the gelatin by soaking in the water for a couple of minutes. Add the boiling water and stir to dissolve the gelatin.
4. Beat in the gelatin mixture to the cream cheese mixture.
5. Add the whipped heavy cream to the cream cheese mixture and stir gently to combine.
6. Pour about 2/3 of the mixture over the base. Using a spatula or spoon, make a well in the center. Spoon the curd into the well.

7. Pour the remaining mixture.

8. Refrigerate for 4 hours, or preferably overnight.
9. Run a knife around the edge of the pan and release the spring on the pan.
10. Decorate the top if desired.
11. Slice and enjoy.

Approximate Nutritional Values Per Serving:
Calories 464 kcal, Protein 8.8 g, Total Fat 45.3 g, Total Carbohydrate 6.3 g, Dietary Fiber 1.6 g, Sugar 4.5 g

CINNAMON BUNDT CAKE

Prep Time 10 minutes
Cook Time 40 minutes
Total Time 50 minutes
Servings 10 slices

Ingredients

Cake
- 7 oz (200 g) Almond Flour (2 cups: Measure by weight if possible)
- 1.5 tbsp Coconut Flour
- 2 tsp Aluminum-Free Baking Powder
- 2 tbsp Ground Cinnamon
- 2 tbsp Stevia Powder
- 5 Large Eggs
- 3 tbsp Melted Coconut Oil (or Unsalted Butter) (Measure melted)
- 3 tbsp Water

Cream Cheese Frosting
- 4 oz (112 g) Cream Cheese, Room Temp
- 1 oz (28 g) Coconut Oil (or Unsalted Butter), Melted
- 4 tbsp Heavy Cream
- 1 tbsp Stevia Powder
- 1 tsp Vanilla Extract
- 2 to 3 tbsp Chopped Nuts (Optional)

Instructions

Cake
1. Preheat the oven to 170 C / 325 F. Grease a 10-inch / 25 cm bundt pan well if not silicone.
2. In a large bowl, whisk well all the dry ingredients.
3. In a separate bowl, beat all the wet ingredients until whitish. Add to the dry mixture and stir with a spatula.
4. Pour the batter into the bundt pan.
5. Bake for 30 - 40 minutes.
6. Let cool on a wire rack.

Cream Cheese Frosting
1. Cream together the cream cheese, coconut oil, heavy cream and stevia.

2. Transfer the mixture to a saucepan and heat it over low for 20 - 30 seconds. Remove from the heat. (* Follow this process if you want to drizzle the frosting over the sides. You can skip it and then spread the frosting with a knife or spatula.)
3. Add the vanilla to the saucepan and mix well.
4. Pour (or spread) the frosting over the cooled cinnamon cake.
5. Sprinkle the chopped nuts.
6. Chill until the frosting is set, or serve immediately. (* Preferably chill the cake overnight so that it gets moister.)

Recipe Notes:
Coconut four varies greatly between brands. If you feel your cake is dry, please reduce the amount next time.

Approximate Nutritional Values Per Serving:
Calories 306 kcal, Protein 9.2 g, Total Fat 28.0 g, Total Carbohydrate 6.2 g, Dietary Fiber 3.0 g, Sugar 1.4 g

CHOCOLATE CHIP BROWNIE TOWER

Prep Time 15 minutes
Cook Time 13 minutes
Total Time 28 minutes
Servings 4

Ingredients

Brownie
- 1 oz (28 g) Unsweetened Baking Chocolate, Chopped
- 1/4 cup (60 cc) Heavy Cream
- 0.88 oz (25 g) Almond Flour (1/4 cup: Measure by weight if possible)
- 1 tbsp Unsweetened Cocoa Powder
- 1 tsp Stevia Powder
- A Pinch of Sea Salt
- 1 Large Egg
- 1 tsp Vanilla Extract
- 3 tbsp (1 oz / 28 g) Sugar Free Chocolate Chips

Chocolate Plate
- 0.5 oz (14 g) Coconut Oil
- 1.5 oz (42 g) Unsweetened Baking Chocolate, Chopped
- 1/2 tsp Liquid Stevia
- 1 tsp Vanilla Extract

Whipped Cream
- 3/4 cup (180 cc) Heavy Cream
- 2 tsp Stevia Powder
- 1 tsp Vanilla Extract
- 1/8 tsp Xanthan Gum (Optional)

To Dust
- 1/2 tsp Unsweetened Cocoa Powder

Instructions

Brownie
1. Preheat the oven to 180 C / 350 F. Line an 8 x 4 inch / 20 x 10 cm loaf pan with parchment paper.

2. Bring the heavy cream to a simmer in a saucepan over low heat. Turn off the heat. Add the unsweetened chocolate. Stir until melted and smooth.
3. In a mixing bowl, add the almond flour, cocoa powder, stevia powder and salt. Whisk well. Add the chocolate mixture and mix well. Add the egg and vanilla extract and mix well. Then, add the chocolate chips and stir lightly.
4. Pour the batter into the prepared loaf pan and level out.
5. Bake for about 10 minutes.
6. Remove from the oven and let cool completely.
7. Cut in half lengthwise and crosswise.

Chocolate Plate
1. Cut parchment paper into a rectangle bigger than a 10-inch / 25 cm square. Fold parchment paper into half, then to the size of the bottom of the loaf pan on both sides of the center line.

2. Melt the coconut oil in a saucepan over low heat. Turn off the heat when half melted. Add the unsweetened chocolate. Leave a couple minutes and then stir until melted. Add the liquid stevia and vanilla, and mix.
3. Pour the chocolate mixture within the folded lines of the parchment paper. Level out.

4. Refrigerate for about 15 minutes, or until set.
5. Remove from the fridge. Cut into 8 rectangles by cutting the whole piece into half along the center line and then each half into half lengthwise and crosswise.

6. Keep them in the fridge until assembly.

Whipped Cream
1. In a large mixing bowl, beat the heavy cream, stevia, vanilla and xanthan gum until stiff peaks form.
2. Place into a large piping bag.

Assembly
1. Pipe the whipped cream on each brownie piece. Then, place a chocolate plate over the cream. Pipe the remaining whipped cream on those chocolate plates and then place each of the remaining chocolate plates over the cream.

2. Dust with the cocoa powder.

Recipe Notes:
Bring to room temperature before serving.
Approximate Nutritional Values Per Serving:
Calories 430 kcal, Protein 7.5 g, Total Fat 44.2 g, Total Carbohydrate 12.2 g, Dietary Fiber 5.2 g, Sugar 2.6 g

NO CRUST BAKED CHEESECAKE WITH BLUEBERRY COMPOTE

Prep Time 10 minutes
Cook Time 55 minutes
Total Time 1 hour 5 minutes
+ Chilling Time
Servings 6 slices

Ingredients

Cheesecake
- 8 oz (227g) Cream Cheese, Softened
- 1 tbsp Stevia Powder
- 7 oz (200 g) Sour Cream, Room Temp
- 2 Eggs, Beaten
- 1/4 tsp Xanthan Gum (Do NOT add too much. The texture would get tofu like)
- 2 tsp Lemon Juice
- 1/2 cup (120 cc) Heavy Cream

Blueberry Compote
- 1/2 cup (55 g) Frozen Blueberries
- 2 tbsp Lemon Juice
- 1/2 tsp Stevia Powder
- 1/2 tsp Chia Seeds

Instructions

Cheesecake
1. Line the base of an 8-inch /20 cm springform pan with parchment paper.
2. Preheat the oven to 160 C / 320 F.
3. In a large bowl, beat the cream cheese and stevia together until smooth.
4. Add the sour cream and beat until smooth.
5. Add 1/2 of the eggs and beat well. Add the remaining 1/2 and beat until well combined.
6. Add the lemon juice, xanthan gum, and heavy cream, beating well between each addition.
7. Pour the batter into the prepared springform pan.
8. Bake for 55 mins.

9. Let cool to room temperature in the pan.
10. Refrigerate in the pan for at least 3 hours until set, or preferably overnight.
11. Run a knife around the cake in the pan to loosen if necessary, and then remove the cake from the pan.
12. Top the chilled cheesecake with the blueberry compote and serve.

Blueberry Compote
1. Add the blueberries to a saucepan and heat the pan over low heat.
2. Stir well and crush them lightly as they begin to release their juice.
3. Add the lemon juice and stevia to the saucepan and stir.
4. Add the chia seeds and stir.
5. Remove the saucepan from heat.
6. Let cool.

Approximate Nutritional Values Per Serving
Sans Blueberry Compote:
Calories 308 kcal, Protein 6.2 g, Total Fat 29.8 g, Total Carbohydrate 2.6 g, Dietary Fiber 0 g, Sugar 2.6 g

DOUBLE CHOCOLATE LAYER CAKE

Prep Time 20 minutes
Cook Time 30 minutes
Total Time 50 minutes
Servings 6

Ingredients

Cake
- 3.5 oz (100 g) Almond Flour (1 cup: Measure by weight if possible)
- 1 tbsp Coconut Flour
- 1.5 tbsp Stevia Powder
- 1 tsp Baking Soda
- A Pinch of Sea Salt
- 3.5 oz (100 g) Coconut Oil (or Unsalted Butter)
- 1/3 cup (80 cc) Water
- 1 oz (28 g) Unsweetened Cocoa Powder
- 2 Eggs
- 1 tsp Vanilla Extract

Chocolate Ganache Frosting
- 3/4 cup (180 cc) Heavy Cream
- 3 oz (85 g) Unsweetened Baking Chocolate, Chopped
- 1.5 tsp Liquid Stevia
- 1 tsp Vanilla Extract

Instructions

Cake
1. Preheat the oven to 180 C / 350 F.
2. Cook the coconut oil, water and cocoa powder in a saucepan over low heat. Stir well until well-combined. Remove from the heat.
3. In a large bowl, mix together the almond flour, coconut flour, stevia, baking soda and salt. Add the chocolate mixture. Mix well until combined.
4. Add the eggs and vanilla and mix well.
5. Pour the batter evenly into 2 different 6-inch / 15 cm round cake pans lined with parchment paper (or silicone pans). (* If you don't have 2 round pans of the

same size, just use a bigger pan. Then, cut the cake in half horizontally.)
6. Bake for 22 - 30 minutes.
7. Let the cakes cool in the pans for about 15 minutes. Then remove from the pans and let cool completely.

Chocolate Ganache Frosting
1. Bring the heavy cream to a simmer in a saucepan over low heat. Turn off the heat.
2. Add the unsweetened chocolate, stevia and vanilla. Stir until melted and smooth.

Assembly
1. Spread about 1/3 of the ganache evenly over one cake layer. Top with the other cake layer.
2. Spread the remaining ganache evenly over top and sides of the cake.
3. Chill at least 30 minutes.

Approximate Nutritional Values Per Serving:
Calories 514 kcal, Protein 9.8 g, Total Fat 51.0 g, Total Carbohydrate 12.8 g, Dietary Fiber 6.1 g, Sugar 2.7 g

RASPBERRY JELLY DOUBLE CHOCOLATE CHEESECAKE

Prep Time 15 minutes
Cook Time 5 minutes
Total Time 20 minutes
+ Chilling Time
Servings 10 slices

Ingredients

Raspberry Jelly
- 5 oz (140 g) Frozen Raspberries
- 3 tbsp Water
- 2 tbsp Lemon Juice
- 1/2 tsp Liquid Stevia
- 0.16 oz (4.5 g) Gelatin (About 1.5 tsp)

Chocolate Mixture
- 1/2 cup (120 cc) Heavy Cream
- 3 oz (85 g) Unsweetened Baking Chocolate, Chopped

Chocolate Cheesecake
- 10 oz (280 g) Cream Cheese, Softened
- 1 tbsp Stevia Powder
- 1 tbsp Vanilla Extract
- 1/2 cup (120 cc) Heavy Cream
- 2 tsp Unsweetened Cocoa Powder (for Light Chocolate Layer)
- 1.5 tbsp Unsweetened Cocoa Powder (for Dark Chocolate Layer)

Instructions

Raspberry Jelly
1. Line a loaf pan with parchment paper. (* The pan shown in the pictures is an 8.5 x 3.6 inch / 22 x 9 cm pan. An 8 x 4 inch / 20 x 10 cm pan also works, but the cake will be much flatter.)
2. Add the frozen raspberries, water, lemon juice and liquid stevia to a saucepan.
3. Stir well and crush them as they begin to release their juice over low heat. Remove the saucepan from the heat once crushed.

4. Quickly strain the seeds out.
5. While still warm, sprinkle the gelatin and stir to dissolve. (* If your gelatin doesn't dissolve in warm liquid, cool the raspberry sauce completely, dissolve the gelatin in it and then warm it in a double boiler or a microwave.)
6. Reserve 1/4 cup (60 cc) into a small bowl. Pour the rest to the prepared loaf pan.

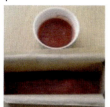

7. Chill for 30 minutes, until set.

Chocolate Cheesecake
1. In a large bowl, beat the heavy cream until soft peaks form. Set aside.
2. In another large bowl, cream the cream cheese using the same hand mixer. Add the stevia and vanilla and beat until smooth and well-combined.
3. Beat in the whipped cream until combined. Then, divide the mixture into 2 equal portions.
4. [For Chocolate Mixture] Bring the heavy cream to a simmer in a saucepan over low heat. Turn off the heat and add the unsweetened chocolate. Stir until melted and smooth.
5. [For Light Chocolate Layer] Add 1/3 of the chocolate mixture to one portion of the cream cheese mixture. Add the 2 teaspoons cocoa powder and beat until well-combined. Transfer the mixture over the raspberry jelly in the loaf pan. Level out and drop the pan a few times. Freeze for about 5 minutes while working on the next steps.
6. [For Dark Chocolate Layer] Add the rest of the chocolate mixture to the remaining cream cheese mixture. Add the 1.5 tablespoons cocoa powder and beat until well-combined.
7. Remove the loaf pan from the freezer and make a trench in the center of the light chocolate layer in the loaf pan, using the handle of a spoon. Spread the mixture removed for the trench over the light chocolate layer on both sides (or eat!).

8. Place the reserved raspberry jelly into a piping bag, then pipe it into the trench. Compress with a spoon if necessary.

9. Transfer the dark chocolate mixture over the light chocolate layer. Level out and drop the pan a few times.
10. Chill for 2 - 3 hours, until set.
11. Invert the loaf pan on a cutting board. Remove the pan. Then remove the parchment paper slowly and carefully because the raspberry jelly may be sticking to the parchment paper.
12. Slice and enjoy. (* Let sit until the cheesecake reaches room temperature if you prefer a creamy texture.).

Approximate Nutritional Values Per Serving:
Calories 231 kcal, Protein 4.3 g, Total Fat 22.6 g, Total Carbohydrate 5.8 g, Dietary Fiber 2.0 g, Sugar 2.4 g

FLOURLESS PEANUT BUTTER CHOCOLATE CAKE

Prep Time 15 minutes
Cook Time 35 minutes
Total Time 50 minutes
Servings 12 pieces

Ingredients

Cake
- 1 cup (240 cc) Heavy Cream
- 2 oz (56 g) Unsalted Butter, Cubed
- 4 oz (112 g) Unsweetened Baking Chocolate, Chopped
- 1/2 cup (140 g) Unsweetened Peanut Butter
- 3 Large Eggs, Separated
- 2 tbsp Stevia Powder
- 1 tsp Baking Soda
- 2 tsp Vanilla Extract
- A Pinch of Sea Salt

Ganache
- 1/3 cup (80 cc) Heavy Cream
- 1.5 oz (42 g) Unsweetened Baking Chocolate, Chopped
- 1 tsp Liquid Stevia
- 1 tsp Vanilla Extract
- 2 tbsp Unsweetened <u>Creamy</u> Peanut Butter

Instructions

Cake

1. Preheat the oven to 180 C / 325 F. Line a cake pan with parchment paper. (* A 10.5 x 7 inch / 26 x 17 cm dish was used for the cake in the pictures. A 9 x 9 inch / 22 x 22 cm dish / pan should work too.)
2. Bring the heavy cream to a simmer in a saucepan over low heat and add the butter. Turn off the heat when the butter is half melted.
3. Add the unsweetened chocolate. Leave a couple minutes and then stir slowly until half melted. Add the peanut butter and stir until melted and smooth. Set aside.

(* If they won't melt, reheat the saucepan over low for about 10 seconds and turn off the heat. Do not overheat.)

4. In a large bowl, whisk well the egg yolks, stevia and baking soda. Add the chocolate mixture and vanilla. Mix well.
5. In a separate bowl, beat the egg whites and salt until stiff peaks form.
6. Add 1/3 of the whites to the chocolate mixture and whisk well. Then gently fold in the remaining whites with a rubber spatula in 2 additions until completely incorporated.
7. Pour the batter into the prepared pan. Smooth the surface.
8. Set a roasting pan on the oven rack. Pour boiling water into the roasting pan to come about halfway up the side of the cake pan.
9. Bake for 23 - 25 minutes. Let the cake sit in the oven for another 10 minutes.
(* The cake will be very moist in the middle.)
10. Remove the cake pan from the water bath and cool to room temperature.

Ganache
1. Bring the heavy cream to a simmer in a saucepan over low heat. Turn off the heat.
2. Add the unsweetened chocolate. Stir until melted and smooth.
3. Add the stevia and vanilla and mix well.

Assembly
1. Heat the peanut butter until a bit melty in a double boiler or in a microwave. Place in a piping bag.
2. Pour and spread the ganache evenly over the top of the cooled cake.
3. Pipe the peanut butter in lines over the still wet ganache. Drag a skewer back and forth across the lines.

4. Chill until set, or dig in!

Approximate Nutritional Values Per Serving:
Calories 322 kcal, Protein 6.6 g, Total Fat 31.8 g, Total Carbohydrate 7.7 g, Dietary Fiber 2.9 g, Sugar 1.4 g

LEMON JELLO CHEESECAKE

Prep Time 25 minutes
Cook Time 10 minutes
Total Time 35 minutes
 + Chilling Time
Servings 8 slices

Ingredients

Crust (For a more flaky almond flour crust, see the Recipe Notes below)
- 1.5 oz (42 g) Coconut Flour (1/3 cup: Measure by weight if possible)
- 1 tsp Stevia Powder
- 1/4 tsp Salt
- 1 Large Egg
- 2 oz (56 g) Unsalted Butter (or Coconut Oil), Melted

No Bake Cheesecake Layer
- 1 tbsp Water
- 2 tsp (6 g) Gelatin
- 2 tbsp Boiling Water
- 8 oz (227 g) Cream Cheese, Softened
- 1.5 tbsp Stevia Powder
- 2 tbsp Lemon Juice
- 1 tsp Vanilla Extract
- 1 cup (240 cc) Heavy Cream

Lemon Jello Layer
- 1 cup (240 cc) Water
- 2 tbsp (20 g) Gelatin
- 1/2 cup (120 cc) Boiling Water
- 1/2 cup (120 cc) Lemon Juice
- 2 tbsp Grated Lemon Zest
- 2 tsp Liquid Stevia (Adjust to your liking)

Instructions

Crust (For a more flaky almond flour crust, see the Recipe Notes below)
1. Preheat the oven to 180 C / 350 F.
2. In a medium bowl, combine the coconut flour, stevia and salt.
3. Add the egg and melted butter and stir until dough comes together.

4. Press evenly into the bottom of an 8-inch / 20 cm springform pan.
5. Prick all over with a fork.
6. Bake for about 10 minutes. (* Do not overbake or it will get hard.)
7. Let cool completely.

No Bake Cheesecake Layer
1. In a small bowl, soften the gelatin by soaking in the water for a couple of minutes. Add the boiling water and stir to dissolve the gelatin. Set aside.
2. In a large bowl, beat the cream cheese, stevia, lemon juice and vanilla until smooth and well-combined. Add the gelatin mixture and beat to combine.
3. In another bowl, beat the heavy cream until thick. (* Stop beating just before soft peaks begin to form.)
4. Fold the whipped heavy cream into the cream cheese mixture.
5. Spread evenly over the cooled crust.
6. Refrigerate for 1 - 2 hours.

Lemon Jello Layer
1. In a large bowl, soften the gelatin by soaking in 1/2 cup of the water for a couple of minutes. Add the boiling water and stir to dissolve the gelatin.
2. Add the remaining water, lemon juice, lemon zest and stevia and mix well.
3. Pour over the cheesecake layer.
4. Refrigerate for 2 - 3 hours or until set. (* Preferably overnight so that the coconut flour crust will get moister.)
5. Run a knife around the edge of the pan and release the spring on the pan.

Recipe Notes:
If you don't like this coconut flour crust, here's a more flaky crust recipe:
- 1 cup + 2 tsp (4.5 oz / 125 g) Almond Flour
- 1 tsp Stevia Powder
- 1/4 tsp Sea Salt
- 1.5 oz (42 g) Unsalted Butter, Melted
Combine all the ingredients. Bake for about 13 minutes at 180 C / 350 F.

Approximate Nutritional Values Per Serving:
Calories 329 kcal, Protein 7.6 g, Total Fat 30.1 g, Total Carbohydrate 6.2 g, Dietary Fiber 1.8 g, Sugar 3.5 g

CHOCOLATE BUTTERCREAM MERINGUE TOWER CAKE

Prep Time 15 minutes
Cook Time 1 hour
Total Time 1 hour 15 minutes
 + Chilling Time
Servings 4

Ingredients

Chocolate Meringue
- 2 Large Egg Whites
- 1/3 cup (40 g) Confectioners Swerve
- 3 tbsp Unsweetened Cocoa Powder
- A Pinch of Stevia Powder
- A Pinch of Cream of Tartar
- 1 tsp Vanilla Extract

Chocolate Buttercream
- 6 oz (170 g) Unsalted Butter, Room Temp
- 1/3 cup (40 g) Confectioners Swerve
- 1/2 tsp Stevia Powder
- 1/3 cup (25 g) Unsweetened Cocoa Powder
- 2 tsp Vanilla Extract
- A Pinch of Sea Salt
- 2 tbsp Heavy Cream
- 5 drops Liquid Stevia (Optional)
- 1/4 tsp Confectioners Swerve (To Dust)

Instructions

Chocolate Meringue
1. Preheat the oven to 120 C / 250 F.
2. Shift together the cocoa, Swerve, stevia and cream of tartar.
3. In a dry bowl, beat the egg whites until soft peaks form.
4. Add in the shifted dry ingredients in 3 parts. Beat to combine between each addition.

5. Add the vanilla.
6. Beat until stiff peaks form.
7. Place the mixture into a piping bag. Pipe 8 3-inch / 7.5 cm disks on a parchment paper lined baking sheet. Pipe the rest into long strips.

8. Bake for 50 - 60 minutes. Turn the oven off, but rest the meringue in the oven for 60 minutes. (* Halfway through the cooling time, open the door for about 5 seconds and close again.)
9. Remove from the oven to cool completely.
10. Carefully remove the meringue disks and strips from the parchment paper using a tool like a turner / spatula.
11. Cut the strips into small pieces (about 1 inch / 2.5 cm). (* Meringue can be made ahead of time and kept in an air tight container.)

Chocolate Buttercream
1. Beat the butter with an electric mixer until pale (about one minute at high speed). Scrape down the sides of the bowl as necessary.
2. Add the Swerve and stevia and beat until fluffy (about 1 - 2 minutes at high speed).
3. Add the cocoa, vanilla and salt. Beat until combined. Scrape down the sides of the bowl as necessary.
4. Add the heavy cream and beat until combined.

5. Optional: Add the liquid stevia and beat until combined.
6. Place into a piping bag.

Assembly (* The recipe yields 2 tower cakes.)
1. Pipe (or spread) 1/8 of the chocolate buttercream on top of a meringue disk. Top with a second meringue disk and pipe the chocolate buttercream again. Repeat with a third and fourth meringue disks. Top with 1/2 of the small meringue pieces.
2. Repeat with the remaining 4 meringue disks, chocolate buttercream and meringue pieces to build another tower.
3. Dust with Swerve.
4. Refrigerate for 1 - 2 hours, or until the chocolate buttercream is set.
5. Slice each in half and serve.

Recipe Notes:
Keep refrigerated. The meringue will soften slightly the longer it sits in the fridge.
Meringue can be made ahead of time. Please keep in an air tight container.
Approximate Nutritional Values Per Serving:
Calories 389 kcal, Protein 3.7 g, Total Fat 40.5 g, Total Carbohydrate 4.4 g, Dietary Fiber 2.2 g, Sugar 2.1 g
(Swerve is not counted as carbs as it doesn't affect blood sugar levels.)

SOUFFLE CUSTARD PIE

Prep Time 20 minutes
Cook Time 38 minutes
Total Time 58 minutes
+ Chilling Time
Servings 6

Ingredients

Crust
- 3.5 oz (100 g) Almond Flour (1 cup: Measure by weight if possible)
- 1 tbsp Coconut Flour
- 1 tsp Stevia Powder
- 1/4 tsp Salt
- 2 oz (56 g) Unsalted Butter, Melted
- 1 tsp Vanilla Extract

Filling
- 2 Egg Yolks
- 1 tbsp Stevia Powder
- 1/4 tsp Xanthan Gum
- 1/2 cup (120 cc) Heavy Cream
- 1 to 3 tsp Vanilla Extract (Adjust to your liking)
- 2 Egg Whites
- 4 oz (112 g) Fresh Strawberries, Halved

Topping (Optional)
- 1 tsp Powdered Sweetener

Instructions

Crust *(* You can make custard cream (Filling - Step 1 - 8) before making a crust.)*
1. Preheat the oven to 180 C / 350 F. Grease a 6-inch / 15 cm tart pan.
2. Combine all the ingredients in a bowl. Mix well until a soft dough forms.
3. Evenly press into the bottom and up the sides of the prepared tart pan.
4. Prick all over with a fork.
5. Bake for 10 minutes.

Filling
1. Whisk the egg yolks and stevia powder in a bowl until pale yellow.
2. Add the xanthan gum. Mix well.

3. Bring the heavy cream to almost a simmer in a saucepan. Then, add to the egg yolk mixture. Quickly whisk to combine, and then transfer the mixture to the saucepan.
4. Keep stirring the mixture with a spatula over low - medium heat. DON'T STOP! When it starts to thicken, stir 20 - 30 more seconds. (* It would only take about 3 minutes to thicken.)
5. Turn off the heat and stir 20 - 30 more seconds. Add the vanilla and mix well.
6. Strain the custard cream through a fine mesh sieve to make it smooth. Pour the custard into a tray and level out.
7. Place a piece of cling wrap over the custard. Stick the wrap to the custard by pressing lightly to prevent a film from forming on top of the custard.
8. Refrigerate for one hour.
9. Remove the custard from the fridge. Remove the wrap carefully and transfer the custard to a bowl.
10. Cream the custard with a whisk. (* Add a little bit of heavy cream if too thick to cream it.)
11. In a separate bowl, beat the egg whites until stiff peaks form.
12. Fold the whites into the custard in 3 parts with a rubber spatula until completely incorporated.

Assembly
1. Preheat the oven to 180 C / 350 F.
2. Pour the filling into the crust and level out.
3. Place the individual strawberry halves on top of the filling.
4. Bake for about 23 minutes for the center to be creamy, OR bake several more minutes if you don't like a creamy texture. (* As ovens vary, check after 20 minutes have passed.)
5. Optional: When cooled, dust with powdered sweetener.
6. Dig in or refrigerate for a couple hours before serving.

Recipe Notes:
You can make custard cream first. Then while chilling the custard cream, make your crust. When the custard cream is ready, start beating egg whites.

You can increase the ingredients and make this pie in a larger tart pan. The more egg whites, the fluffier. **However**, please be aware that that may make your strawberries sink in and disappear from the surface while baking. Also, a much longer period of baking time will be required. So, sticking to the recipe is recommended.

Approximate Nutritional Values Per Serving:
Calories 302 kcal, Protein 6.9 g, Total Fat 28.1 g, Total Carbohydrate 7.1 g, Dietary Fiber 2.9 g, Sugar 2.8 g

ALMOND BUTTER CHOCOLATE PIE

Prep Time 15 minutes
Cook Time 20 minutes
Total Time 35 minutes
+ Chilling Time
Servings 14 slices

Ingredients

Crust
- 6.17 oz (175 g) Almond Flour (1 3/4 cups: Measure by weight if possible)
- 1/3 cup (30 g) Unsweetened Cocoa Powder
- 1 tsp Stevia Powder
- 1 tsp Ground Cinnamon
- 1/4 tsp Salt
- 1 tsp Vanilla Extract
- 2.5 oz (70 g) Unsalted Butter, Melted

Almond Butter Layer
- 1 cup (240 cc) Heavy Cream (* 1/2 cup for the chocolate layer)
- 1/6 tsp Salt
- 3 oz (85 g) Unsalted Butter, Room Temp
- 2/3 cup (180 g) Almond Butter, Room Temp
- 1 tsp Stevia Powder

Chocolate Layer
- 3/4 cup (180 cc) Heavy Cream
- 4 oz (112 g) Unsweetened Baking Chocolate, Chopped
- 1 tbsp Vanilla Extract
- 2 tsp Liquid Stevia

Whipped Cream Layer
- 1 cup (240 cc) Heavy Cream
- 3/4 tbsp Stevia Powder
- 1 tsp Vanilla Extract

Topping
- 1/2 tsp Unsweetened Cocoa Powder

Instructions

Crust
1. Preheat the oven to 180 C / 350 F. Grease a 9-inch / 22 cm tart pie pan with a removable bottom or line with parchment paper. (* The pan used for the pie in the pictures is about 1.8 inch / 4.5 cm deep.)
2. In a mixing bowl, whisk well the dry ingredients. Add the vanilla and melted butter and stir until dough comes together.
3. Press evenly into the bottom and up the sides of the pan.
4. Prick all over with a fork.
5. Bake for about 18 minutes.
6. Let cool completely.

Almond Butter Layer
1. In a large bowl, beat the heavy cream and salt until medium peaks form. Set aside.
2. In a separate bowl, cream the butter with the same hand mixer. Add the almond butter and stevia powder and beat to combine.
3. Fold in 1/2 of the whipped cream. (* Reserve the other 1/2 in the fridge for the chocolate layer.)
4. Spread evenly over the cooled crust.
5. Refrigerate for 15 - 30 minutes.

Chocolate Layer
1. Bring the heavy cream to a simmer in a saucepan over low heat. Turn off the heat.
2. Add the unsweetened chocolate. Stir until melted and smooth.
3. Add the vanilla and liquid stevia and mix well.
4. Make sure the chocolate mixture is not hot and transfer to a bowl. Fold in the reserved whipped cream. (* Use a whisk if necessary.)
5. Spread evenly over the almond butter mixture.
6. Refrigerate for 1 - 1.5 hours or until set.

Whipped Cream Layer
1. Add all the ingredients to a mixing bowl and beat until stiff peaks form.
2. Place into a piping bag and pipe over the chocolate layer, or just spread onto the chocolate layer.

Topping
1. Dust with the cocoa powder.

Recipe Notes:
Keep refrigerated. Let stand for 5 - 15 minutes at room temp before serving if you like it melty.

Approximate Nutritional Values Per Serving:
Calories 482 kcal, Protein 7.8 g, Total Fat 48.0 g, Total Carbohydrate 10.4 g, Dietary Fiber 4.5 g, Sugar 2.7 g

VANILLA CUSTARD CHOCOLATE TARTLETS

Prep Time 30 minutes
Cook Time 20 minutes
Total Time 50 minutes
+ Chilling Time
Servings 6 tartlets

Ingredients

Crust
- 5.3 oz (150 g) Almond Flour (1 1/2 cups: Measure by weight if possible)
- 1 tsp Stevia Powder
- 1/4 tsp Salt
- 2 oz (56 g) Unsalted Butter, Melted
- 1 tsp Vanilla Extract

Custard Layer
- 3 Egg Yolks
- 1 tbsp Stevia Powder
- 3/4 cup (180 cc) Heavy Cream
- 1/4 tsp Xanthan Gum
- 1 to 3 tsp Vanilla Extract (Adjust to your liking. 3 teaspoons are recommended)

Chocolate Layer
- 1/3 cup (80 cc) Heavy Cream
- 0.5 oz (14 g) Unsweetened Baking Chocolate, Chopped
- 2 tsp Unsweetened Cocoa Powder
- 1.5 tsp Liquid Stevia
- 1 tsp Vanilla Extract

Topping (Optional)
- Finely Chopped Nuts, etc

Instructions

Crust
1. Preheat the oven to 180 C / 350 F. Grease each cavity of your muffin pan if not silicone. (* Silicon is highly recommended.)
2. Combine well all the ingredients in a bowl until a soft dough forms.

3. Divide the dough into 6 equal portions and evenly press each into the bottom and up the sides of the prepared muffin pan.
4. Prick the bottom of each tart with a fork.
5. Bake for 10 - 12 minutes.
6. Let them cool to room temperature, and then transfer to the fridge.

Vanilla Custard Layer
1. Whisk the egg yolks and stevia powder in a bowl until pale yellow.
2. Add the xanthan gum. Mix well.
3. Bring the heavy cream to almost a simmer in a saucepan. Add to the egg yolk mixture. QUICKLY whisk to combine, and then transfer the mixture to the saucepan.
4. Keep stirring the mixture with a spatula over low - medium heat. DON'T STOP! When it starts to thicken, stir 20 - 30 more seconds. (* It only takes 3 - 4 minutes to thicken.)
5. Turn off the heat and stir 20 - 30 more seconds. Add the vanilla extract and mix well.
6. Strain the custard cream through a fine mesh sieve to make it smooth. Pour the custard into a tray and level out.
7. Place a piece of cling wrap over the custard. Stick the cling wrap to the custard by pressing lightly to prevent a film from forming on top of the custard as it cools.
8. Refrigerate for about one hour.
9. Remove the custard from the fridge. Remove the wrap carefully and transfer the custard to a bowl.
10. Cream the custard with a whisk. (* Add a little bit of heavy cream if too thick to cream it.)
11. Spoon the custard into each tartlet. Level out if necessary.
12. Refrigerate while making the chocolate layer.

Chocolate Layer
1. Bring the heavy cream to a simmer in a saucepan over low heat. Turn off the heat.
2. Add the unsweetened chocolate and cocoa. Stir until melted and smooth.
3. Add the stevia and vanilla and mix well.
4. Spoon the chocolate mixture over the custard filling. (* You might want to place the silicone muffin pan on a tray before spooning so that the chocolate layer won't overflow while transferring to the fridge.)

To Serve
1. Sprinkle the topping if desired.
2. Refrigerate for about 20 minutes or until the chocolate is set to your liking.
3. Remove from the fridge. Carefully remove each tartlet from the muffin pan.

Recipe Notes:
Keep refrigerated. Eat within 2 - 3 days.
Approximate Nutritional Values Per Serving:
Calories 472 kcal, Protein 9.0 g, Total Fat 46.1 g, Total Carbohydrate 8.6 g, Dietary Fiber 3.6 g, Sugar 2.6 g

BUTTERY ALMOND TARTLETS

Prep Time 15 minutes
Cook Time 25 minutes
Total Time 40 minutes
Servings 5 tartlets

Ingredients

Crust
- 4.4 oz (125 g) Almond Flour (1 cup + 2 tbsp: Measure by weight if possible)
- 1 tsp Stevia Powder
- 1/4 tsp Salt
- 1.5 oz (42 g) Unsalted Butter, Melted

Almond Cream Filling
- 2 oz (56 g) Unsalted Butter, Room Temp or Lightly Softened
- 1/2 tbsp Stevia Powder
- 2 oz (56 g) Egg, Beaten (One egg should be about 2 oz / 56 g)
- 2 oz (56 g) Almond Flour, Sifted (1/2 cup: Measure by weight if possible)

Toppings
- Sliced Almonds, Blueberries, etc

Instructions

Crust
1. Preheat the oven to 170 C / 325 F. Grease each cavity of your muffin pan well if not silicone. (* Silicone is recommended.)
2. Whisk the almond flour, stevia and salt in a bowl.
3. Add the melted butter and mix well until a soft dough forms.
4. Divide the dough into 5 equal portions and evenly press each into the bottom and up the sides of the muffin pan.
5. Prick the bottom of each tart with a fork.
6. Bake for 10 minutes.
7. Let them cool to room temperature.

Almond Cream Filling
1. Cream the butter in a bowl with a spatula and then a wire whisk, trying NOT to overbeat. (* Do not use an electric hand mixer.) Otherwise, air bubbles will be created and the filling will puff up while baking.
2. Add the sweetener and mix gently.
3. Add the egg in 3 parts. Mix well between each addition.
4. Add the almond flour and stir well.

Assembly
1. Preheat the oven to 170 C / 325 F.
2. Spoon the filling into each tartlet.
3. Drop the muffin pan several times to flatten out the filling and to get the air bubbles out.
4. Sprinkle your toppings on the filling.
5. Bake for 13 - 15 minutes.
6. Let them cool completely and carefully remove from the muffin pan.

Recipe Notes:
They taste better after overnight refrigeration. Bring to room temp before serving.

Approximate Nutritional Values Per Serving:
Calories 396 kcal, Protein 10 g, Total Fat 37.6 g, Total Carbohydrate 8.8 g, Dietary Fiber 4.3 g, Sugar 1.5 g

PEANUT BUTTER CHOCOLATE MOUSSE TART

Prep Time 25 minutes
Cook Time 15 minutes
Total Time 40 minutes
+ Chilling Time
Servings 6

Ingredients

Crust (For a more flaky almond flour crust, see the Recipe Notes below)
- 1.76 oz (50 g) Coconut Flour (1/2 cup: Measure by weight if possible)
- 1/4 tsp Salt
- 1/2 tsp Stevia Powder (Optional)
- 1 Egg
- 2.47 oz (70 g) Coconut Oil (or Unsalted Butter), Melted

Peanut Butter Layer
- 1/2 cup (140 g) Unsweetened Peanut Butter
- 2 oz (56 g) Cream Cheese
- 1 tsp Ground Cinnamon
- 1 tsp Stevia Powder
- 1/2 cup (120 cc) Heavy Cream

Chocolate Mousse Layer
- 1 tbsp Water
- 1.5 tsp Gelatin
- 1.5 tbsp Boiling Water
- 3 tbsp Unsweetened Cocoa Powder
- 1/2 to 1 tbsp Stevia Powder (Adjust)
- 1/2 cup (120 cc) Heavy Cream
- 1 tsp Vanilla Extract

Topping
- 1 to 2 tsp Sugar Free Chocolate, Grated

Instructions

Crust
1. Preheat the oven to 180 C / 350 F. Butter a 6-inch / 15 cm tart pan.
2. In a medium bowl, combine the coconut flour, salt and stevia.
3. Add the egg and melted coconut oil and stir until dough comes together.
4. Press evenly into the bottom and up the sides of the tart pan.
5. Prick all over with a fork.
6. Bake for 13 - 15 minutes.
7. Let cool completely.

Peanut Butter Layer
1. Mix all the peanut butter layer ingredients with an electric mixer or in a food processor until smooth and well-combined.
2. Spread evenly over the cooled crust.
3. Refrigerate for 30 - 60 minutes.

Chocolate Mousse layer
1. In a small bowl, soften the gelatin by soaking in the water for a couple of minutes. Add the boiling water and stir to dissolve the gelatin and set aside.
2. In a separate medium bowl, add the rest of the ingredients and beat until hard. Add the gelatin mixture and beat until well-combined.
3. Spread over the peanut butter layer.
4. Refrigerate for 30 - 60 minutes.

To Serve
1. Sprinkle the grated chocolate on top.
2. Carefully remove from the pan.
3. Slice and enjoy.

Recipe Notes:
If you don't like this coconut flour crust, here's a more flaky crust recipe:
- 1 1/3 cup (5.3 oz / 150 g) Almond Flour
- 1 tsp Stevia Powder
- 1/4 tsp Sea Salt
- 2 oz (56 g) Unsalted Butter, Melted
- 1tsp Vanilla Extract

Combine all the ingredients. Bake for about 12 - 15 minutes at 180 C / 350 F.

Approximate Nutritional Values Per Serving:
Calories 496 kcal, Protein 10.9 g, Total Fat 46.0 g, Total Carbohydrate, 12.5 g, Dietary Fiber 5.7 g, Sugar 4.7 g

CHOCOLATE ÉCLAIR CUPS WITH CARAMEL SAUCE

Prep Time 20 minutes
Cook Time 30 minutes
Total Time 50 minutes
+ Chilling Time
Servings 8 cups

Ingredients

Chocolate Custard Cream Layer
- 3 Egg Yolks
- 1 tbsp Stevia Powder
- 3/4 cup (180 cc) Heavy Cream
- 1/4 tsp Xanthan Gum
- 2 to 3 tsp Vanilla Extract
- 1 oz (28 g) Unsweetened Baking Chocolate, Finely Chopped
- 1 tsp Heavy Cream (Optional: To be added after one hour refrigeration)

Fat Head Cups
- 1 1/2 cups (160 g) Shredded Mozzarella Cheese
- 2 oz (56 g) Cream Cheese
- 1 Egg
- 4 tbsp (30 g) Coconut Flour (OR 3 oz (85 g) Almond Flour)
- 1/2 tsp Stevia Powder
- 1/2 tsp Aluminum-Free Baking Powder
- 1/2 tsp Xanthan Gum
- 1/2 tsp Ground Cinnamon

Whipped Cream Layer
- 1/2 cup (120 cc) Heavy Cream
- 1 tsp Stevia Powder
- 1 tsp Vanilla Extract
- A Pinch of Sea Salt

Caramel Sauce
- 1 tbsp (14 g) Unsalted Butter
- 3 tbsp Confectioners Swerve
- 1/4 cup (60 cc) Heavy Cream
- A Pinch of Xanthan Gum
- 1 tsp Heavy Cream (or Water)

Toppings (Optional)
- Chopped Nuts, Sliced Almonds, etc

Instructions

Chocolate Custard Cream
1. Whisk the egg yolks and stevia powder in a bowl until pale yellow.
2. Add the xanthan gum. Mix well.
3. Bring the heavy cream to almost a simmer in a saucepan. Add to the egg yolk mixture. QUICKLY whisk to combine, and then transfer the mixture to the saucepan.
4. Keep stirring the mixture with a spatula over low - medium heat. DON'T STOP!
5. When it starts to thicken, turn off the heat and stir 20 - 30 more seconds. Add the vanilla extract and mix well. (* It doesn't have to be very thick here because the chocolate will be added and the custard will be thicker after refrigeration anyway.)
6. Strain the custard through a fine mesh sieve to make it smooth. Add the unsweetened chocolate while still hot and let sit for a couple of minutes. Stir well until melted and creamy.
7. Place a piece of cling wrap over the chocolate custard. Stick the wrap to the custard by pressing lightly to prevent a film from forming on top of the custard.
8. Refrigerate for about one hour.

Fat Head Cups
1. Preheat the oven to 190 C / 375 F. Grease your muffin pan if not silicone.
2. In a large saucepan, melt the mozzarella cheese and cream cheese over low heat until it can be stirred together and remove from the heat. (Or microwave 1 - 1.5 minutes.)
3. Stir until well combined.
4. Add the egg and stir.
5. Add the rest of the ingredients and mix well.
6. Wet your hand and knead well until uniform. (* Reheat the dough if it gets crumbly. Add flour little by little (like 1/2 tsp at a time) if the dough is too sticky.)
7. Divide the dough into 8 equal portions and press each into the bottom and up the sides of the prepared muffin pan. (* Wetting your hands helps.)
8. Bake for about 18 minutes (* a couple of minutes shorter if not silicone).
9. Remove from the oven. Carefully with the back of a spoon, press the center back down if they have puffed.
10. Remove from the pan and let cool completely on a wire rack.

Whipped Cream Layer
1. Add all the ingredients into a mixing bowl and beat until stiff peaks form.
2. Place into a piping bag. Transfer to the fridge.

Caramel Sauce
1. In a saucepan over medium - low heat, combine the butter and Swerve. Bring to a boil, stir occasionally as needed and cook until browned (about 3 - 5 minutes). Turn off the heat.
2. Add one teaspoon of the heavy cream. The mixture will rapidly bubble. When it ceases, add the remaining heavy cream. Stir over medium - low heat until it thickens.
3. Turn off the heat and sprinkle with the xanthan gum. Whisk well to combine.
4. Turn on the heat again and stir over medium - low heat for about 20 - 30 seconds or until it gets thicker. Turn off the heat.
5. Add the heavy cream (or water) and mix well.

Assembly
1. Remove the chocolate custard from the fridge. Remove the wrap carefully. Cream it with a whisk. (* Optional: Add the heavy cream if too thick to cream it.) Spoon the chocolate custard evenly into each cup.
2. Pipe the whipped cream over the chocolate custard.
3. Place the caramel sauce into a piping bag and pipe over the whipped cream. (* If the caramel sauce has crystalized, stir over low heat gently until creamy.)
4. Optional: Sprinkle your toppings on top.
5. Refrigerate overnight if possible, or serve immediately.

Recipe Notes:
They taste better after overnight refrigeration rather than serving right away.
Make chocolate custard cream and fat head cups first, and then put the custard into the cups and chill overnight. On the following day, make whipped cream and caramel sauce. (Or you can make them all and build up in one day, and chill overnight.)

Approximate Nutritional Values Per Serving:
Calories 371 kcal, Protein 10.2 g, Total Fat 34.0 g, Total Carbohydrate 5.9 g, Dietary Fiber 2.1 g, Sugar 2.2 g
(Swerve is not counted as carbs as it doesn't affect blood sugar levels.)

NO-CHURN AVOCADO STRAWBERRY PROTEIN ICE CREAM

Prep Time 8 minutes
Total Time 8 minutes
+ Chilling Time
Servings 4 scoops

Ingredients
- 3 oz (85 g) Frozen Strawberries
- 1/2 Avocado, Peeled & Pitted
- 1 tsp Lemon Juice
- 1/2 cup (120 cc) Heavy Cream
- 1 tsp Liquid Stevia (Replace some with berry flavored stevia if desired)
- 1 tbsp Vanilla Extract
- 3 tbsp (18 g) Whey Protein Powder
- 2 Frozen Strawberries for Toppings, Lightly Thawed and Cut into Tiny Pieces

Instructions
1. Mix the strawberries, avocado, and lemon juice in a food processor / blender until smooth and creamy.
2. In a mixing bowl, beat the heavy cream, stevia and vanilla until stiff peaks form. Add the strawberry avocado mixture and the protein powder. Stir well with a spatula to combine.
3. Transfer the mixture to a freezer safe container, cover and freeze for a total of 4 - 5 hours. (* Remove from the freezer about 30 minutes after and whisk well. Transfer back to the freezer. Wait another 30 minutes and repeat. Then repeat one more time.)
4. Sprinkle the strawberries (the juice too).

Recipe Notes:
This ice cream won't get rock hard in the freezer even after longer periods, but if it does, let it sit out at room temp for a few minutes.

Approximate Nutritional Values Per Serving:
Calories 193 kcal, Protein 4.6 g, Total Fat 17.6 g, Total Carbohydrate 4.9 g, Dietary Fiber 1.4 g, Sugar 3.3 g

CHOCOLATE DIPPED ICE CREAM TACOS (HOMEMADE CHOCO TACO)

Prep Time 30 minutes
Cook Time 7 minutes
Total Time 37 minutes
+ Chilling Time
Servings 4 - 5 tacos

Ingredients

Taco Shells
- 0.75 oz (21 g) Almond Flour
- 5 tsp Unsweetened Cocoa Powder
- 1/4 tsp Xanthan Gum
- 1 oz (28 g) Unsalted Butter, Softened
- 1.5 tsp Stevia Powder
- 1 Large Egg
- 1 tsp Vanilla

Chocolate Coating
- 1.25 oz (35 g) Coconut Oil
- 3 oz (85 g) Unsweetened Baking Chocolate, Chopped
- 1.5 tsp Liquid Stevia
- 2 tsp Vanilla Extract

Vanilla Ice Cream
- 3/4 cup (180 cc) Heavy Cream
- 2 tsp Stevia Powder
- 2 tsp Vanilla Extract

Topping
- 1 oz (28 g) Salted Peanuts, Crushed

Instructions

Taco Shells
1. Preheat the oven to 180 C / 350 F.
2. In a bowl, whisk well the almond flour, cocoa and xanthan gum.
3. In a separate bowl, beat the butter and stevia. Add the almond flour mixture, egg and vanilla and beat well to combine.
4. Divide the dough into 4 equal portions (or 5 portions if desired) and place on a baking sheet lined with parchment paper. Spread each portion into a 5-inch / 12.5 cm circle (or smaller if dividing into 5 portions), using the back of a wet spoon. (* Wet your spoon whenever necessary because the dough is very gooey.)

5. Bake for 6 - 7 minutes. (* Do not overbake.)
6. Remove from the oven. Carefully lift each warm disc and drape over the edge of a loaf pan (or in any other way that works), making the baked side the outside of a shell. Let set for 15 minutes, then freeze for 30 minutes.

Chocolate Coating
1. Melt the coconut oil in a saucepan over low heat. Turn off the heat when half melted.
2. Add the unsweetened chocolate. Leave a couple minutes and then stir until melted. Add the liquid stevia and vanilla, and mix.

3. Remove the taco shells from the freezer. Coat the inside of each taco shell with the chocolate, using a spoon or brush. Then, freeze for 10 minutes or until set. Reserve the rest of the chocolate for later.

Vanilla Ice Cream
1. In a large mixing bowl, beat the heavy cream, stevia and vanilla until stiff peaks form.
2. Place into a large piping bag. Remove the taco shells from the freezer and fill each shell with the whipped cream. Push it even with the rim of the shell, using a butter knife.
3. Freeze for 2 - 3 hours.

Final Assembly
1. Re-melt the reserved chocolate over low heat if necessary. (* You may want to turn off the heat when 1/3 is melted, and then leave a couple minutes.) Remove the tacos from the freezer and dip the top of each taco in the chocolate and sprinkle with the crushed peanuts.

2. Freeze again to set the chocolate for 20 - 30 minutes.

Approximate Nutritional Values Per Serving:
- Per Taco When Making 4 Tacos:
  Calories 494 kcal, Protein 8.0 g, Total Fat 50.8 g, Total Carbohydrate 11.6 g, Dietary Fiber 4.9 g, Sugar 2.4 g
  (One taco is pretty big when making only 4, so please stop eating where you've met your macros, if you can.)
- Per Taco When Making 5 Tacos:
  Calories 395 kcal, Protein 6.4 g, Total Fat 40.6 g, Total Carbohydrate 9.2 g, Dietary Fiber 3.9 g, Sugar 1.9 g

AVOCADO BERRY COCONUT CREAM POPSICLES

Prep Time 5 minutes
Total Time 5 minutes
+ Chilling Time
Servings 5 pops

Ingredients
- 1 Ripe Avocado, Peeled & Pitted
- 3.5 oz (100 g) Fresh Berries
- 6.8 fl oz (200 ml) Coconut Cream
- 1 tbsp Lemon Juice
- 1 tsp Liquid Stevia

Instructions
1. Mix all the ingredients in a food processor / blender until smooth and creamy.
2. Spoon the mixture into 5 popsicle molds.
3. Tap the filled popsicle molds on the counter top and place popsicle sticks into the mixture.
4. Freeze for 3 - 4 hours.

Recipe Notes:
The popsicles will get hard in the freezer after longer periods, but not rock hard. Let them sit out at room temp for a few minutes before serving. Instead of coconut cream, you can use coconut milk. However, the popsicles will be much icier and a bit harder to bite, so you may need to let them sit out at room temp a bit longer.
If you don't have a popsicle mold, you can spoon the mixture into small silicone cups and enjoy like fat bombs.

Approximate Nutritional Values Per Serving
When Using Strawberries**:**
Calories 166 kcal, Protein 1.9 g, Total Fat 16.4 g, Total Carbohydrate 4.6 g, Dietary Fiber 2.4 g, Sugar 2.8 g

NO-CHURN PEANUT BUTTER ICE CREAM

Prep Time 10 minutes
Cook Time 1 minute
Total Time 11 minutes
+ Chilling Time
Servings 4 - 6

Ingredients

Ice Cream
- 6 oz (170 g) Cream Cheese, Room Temp
- 5 tbsp Unsweetened Peanut Butter
- 1 tbsp Stevia Powder
- 1.5 tsp Vanilla Extract
- 3/4 cup (180 cc) Heavy Cream

Chocolate Hot Fudge Sauce
- 1/4 cup (60 cc) Heavy Cream
- 1 oz (28 g) Unsweetened Baking Chocolate, Chopped
- 1 tsp Liquid Stevia
- 1 tsp Vanilla Extract

Instructions

Ice Cream
1. In a large bowl, mix together the cream cheese, peanut butter, stevia and vanilla.
2. In another bowl, beat the heavy cream until stiff peaks form.
3. Fold in the whipped cream to the cream cheese mixture.
4. Transfer the mixture to a freezer safe container, cover it, and freeze for 4 - 5 hours.
5. Pour the chocolate hot fudge sauce over the ice cream before serving.

Chocolate Hot Fudge Sauce
1. Bring the heavy cream to a simmer in a saucepan over low heat. Remove from the heat.
2. Add the unsweetened chocolate and stevia. Stir until melted and smooth.
3. Add the vanilla and mix well.

Recipe Notes:
Ice cream will get hard in the freezer after longer periods, but not rock hard. Let it sit out at room temp for a few minutes before serving.

Approximate Nutritional Values Per Serving:
- 1/4
  Calories 500 kcal, Protein 9.4 g, Total Fat 49.9 g, Total Carbohydrate 8.3 g, Dietary Fiber 2.2 g, Sugar 3.3 g
- 1/6:
  Calories 333 kcal, Protein 6.2 g, Total Fat 33.2 g, Total Carbohydrate 5.5 g, Dietary Fiber 1.5 g, Sugar 2.2 g

TIRAMISU POPSICLES

Prep Time 10 minutes
Cook Time 20 minutes
Total Time 30 minutes
+ Chilling Time
Servings 7 pops

Ingredients

Cookie
- 1.76 oz (50 g) Almond Flour (About 1/2 cup: Measure by weight if possible)
- 1 tsp Coconut Flour
- 1/2 tsp Stevia Powder
- A Pinch of Sea Salt
- 1 oz (28 g) Unsalted Butter
- 1 tsp Instant Coffee Granules
- 1/2 tsp Vanilla Extract

Popsicle Mixture
- 1/2 cup (120 cc) Heavy Cream
- 6.5 oz (185 g) Mascarpone Cheese, Room Temp
- 2 tsp Liquid Stevia
- 1 tsp Vanilla Extract
- 1.5 tsp Instant Coffee Granules

To Dust
- 1 tsp Unsweetened Cocoa Powder

Instructions

Cookie
1. Preheat the oven to 180 C / 350 F.
2. Melt the butter, then add the instant coffee and mix well. (* It's okay even if the granules won't dissolve fully.)
3. In a mixing bowl, whisk well the almond flour, coconut flour, stevia powder and salt. Add the butter mixture and vanilla. Stir until a soft dough forms.

4. Spread the dough into a 5-inch / 12.5 cm square on a baking sheet lined with parchment paper.

5. Bake for 20 minutes.
6. Let cool completely on a wire rack.
7. When cooled, place in a reusable plastic bag and seal. Crush with a rolling pin. (* The cookie is probably brittle, so if you want chunks in your popsicles, don't crush vigorously.)
8. Set aside.

Popsicle Mixture
1. In a large bowl, beat the heavy cream until stiff peaks form. Set aside.
2. In another large bowl, beat the mascarpone until creamy. Beat in the liquid stevia, vanilla and instant coffee. Fold in the whipped cream. Then add the crushed cookies in 2 parts, mixing after each.
3. Spoon the mixture into an Egg Bites Mold which should have 7 holes (or into any other silicone mold), then tap the mold onto the counter top to even out. Insert popsicle sticks.

4. Freeze for at least 3 hours.
5. Remove the popsicles from the mold.
6. Dust with the cocoa powder RIGHT BEFORE serving.

Recipe Notes:
If your popsicles get rock hard in the freezer after longer periods, let sit out at room temp for a couple minutes.
You can use any silicone molds. Removing these popsicles from non-silicone molds may not be easy as silicone molds.

Approximate Nutritional Values Per Serving
Calories 258 kcal, Protein 4.1 g, Total Fat 25.8 g, Total Carbohydrate 3.3 g, Dietary Fiber 1.0 g, Sugar 1.7 g

FROZEN PUMPKIN BITES

Prep Time 10 minutes
Total Time 10 minutes
+ Chilling Time
Servings 10 bites

Ingredients
- 6 oz (170 g) Cream Cheese
- 1/3 cup (85 g) Pumpkin Puree
- 1 tsp Ground Cinnamon
- 1 tsp Stevia Powder
- 3 tbsp (18 g) Whey Protein Powder (See the Recipe Notes below)
- A Pinch of Sea Salt
- 1.5 tsp Vanilla Extract
- 10 Pumpkin Seeds (Optional)

Instructions
1. In a large bowl, beat the cream cheese and pumpkin puree with an electric mixer until combined and smooth.
2. Add the cinnamon, stevia, whey protein, salt and vanilla and beat until combined.
3. Cut cling wrap (about 6 inch / 15 cm long). Place a generous tablespoon of the mixture in the center of the cling wrap. (* The recipe should yield 10 pieces.) Gather the edges of the cling wrap to shape the mixture into a tiny pumpkin and twist the end. (* Make sure to not twist tight.) Repeat with the remaining mixture.

4. Freeze 2 - 3 hours. (* Remove them from the freezer to reshape about 30 minutes after you transfer to the freezer, if necessary.)
5. Remove from the freezer. Remove the cling wraps. (* You may need to work fast.)
6. Optional: Stick a pumpkin seed on the top of each piece.

Recipe Notes:
If your frozen pumpkin bites get hard after longer periods in the freezer, let them sit out at room temp for a couple of minutes.
Even if you don't serve them right away, remove the cling wraps after 3 hours of freezing and then store in an air tight container in the freezer.
Whey protein powder is added to give the frozen pieces a milk taste as well as to prevent them from getting icy. If you don't like to add whey protein, you can omit, but they may get a bit icy.

Approximate Nutritional Values Per Serving:
Calories 69 kcal, Protein 2.8 g, Total Fat 5.8 g, Total Carbohydrate 1.4 g, Dietary Fiber 0.4 g, Sugar 0.7 g

MERINGUE COOKIE PEANUT BUTTER CHOCOLATE BARS

Prep Time 10 minutes
Cook Time 1 hour 2 minutes
Total Time 1 hour 12 minutes
+ Chilling Time
Servings 16

Ingredients

Meringue Cookies
- 1 Egg White
- 3 tbsp Confectioners Swerve
- A Pinch of Stevia Powder (Optional)
- 1/2 tsp Vanilla Extract

Chocolate
- 3/4 cup (180 cc) Heavy Cream
- 4 oz (112 g) Unsalted Butter, Cubed
- 3 oz (85 g) Unsweetened Baking Chocolate, Chopped
- 1/3 cup (80 g) Unsweetened Creamy Peanut Butter, Room Temp
- 1 tsp Liquid Stevia
- 2 tsp Vanilla Extract

Instructions

Meringue Cookies
1. Preheat the oven to 120 C / 250 F.
2. In a dry bowl, beat the egg white until soft peaks form.
3. Mix the Swerve and stevia in a tiny bowl. Add to the egg white in 3 parts. Beat to combine between each addition. Add the vanilla in the last addition. Beat until stiff peaks form.
4. Place the mixture into a piping bag. Pipe 3/4-inch / 2 cm round cookies onto a baking sheet lined with parchment paper. (* It should yield 60 - 70 cookies.)
5. Bake for 60 minutes. Turn the oven off but leave in the oven for 30 - 60 minutes.
6. Remove from the oven to cool completely.

Chocolate
1. Bring 1/2 of the heavy cream to a simmer in a saucepan over low heat.
2. Add the butter. Remove from the heat when the butter is half melted.
3. Add the unsweetened chocolate. Leave 3 - 5 minutes and then stir slowly until melted.
4. Add the remaining heavy cream and stir slowly until combined.
5. Add the peanut butter, stevia and vanilla. Then stir slowly until combined.

Assembly
1. Spoon about 5 tablespoons of the chocolate mixture onto an 8-inch / 20 cm square pan lined with parchment paper. Spread.
2. Place the meringue cookies over the chocolate mixture.

3. Pour the remaining chocolate mixture. Smooth the surface.
4. Freeze for about 60 minutes, or until set.
5. Remove from the freezer. Slice and serve.

Recipe Notes:
Keep in the freezer. Let sit out 1 - 5 minutes at room temperature before serving so that the chocolate gets a bit melty and you can still get the crisp texture of meringue cookies. (* Keeping in the fridge makes the texture of the meringue cookies too soft.)

Approximate Nutritional Values Per Serving:
Calories 163 kcal, Protein 2.2 g, Total Fat 16.7 g, Total Carbohydrate 3.0 g, Dietary Fiber 1.2 g, Sugar 0.6 g
(Swerve is not counted as carbs as it doesn't affect blood sugar levels.)

MELT-IN-YOUR-MOUTH CHOCOLATE FUDGE

Prep Time 3 minutes
Cook Time 2 minute
Total Time 5 minutes
+ Chilling Time
Servings 24 pieces

Ingredients
- 3 oz (85 g) Coconut Oil
- 2 oz (56 g) Unsweetened Baking Chocolate, Chopped
- 1/2 cup (120 cc) Heavy Cream
- 1.5 tsp Liquid Stevia
- 1 tsp Vanilla Extract
- 1 tsp Unsweetened Cocoa Powder (Optional: To Dust)

Instructions
1. Melt the coconut oil in a saucepan over low heat.
2. Remove from the heat when it's about 3/4 melted.
3. Add the unsweetened chocolate to the saucepan. Let stand a couple minutes and then stir until melted and creamy.
4. Add the heavy cream. While stirring, reheat the saucepan about 10 - 15 second and remove from the heat. (* Do NOT overheat to avoid oil separation.)
5. Add the liquid stevia and vanilla and stir well.
6. Pour into a silicone mold or a pan lined with parchment paper.
7. Freeze for 1.5 - 2 hours.
8. Remove from the pan and slice into 24 pieces.
9. Optional: Dust the fudge with cocoa powder.

Recipe Notes:
Keep them in the fridge or freezer.
Approximate Nutritional Values Per Serving:
Calories 67 kcal, Protein 0.5 g, Total Fat 7.1 g, Total Carbohydrate 1.1 g, Dietary Fiber 0.5 g, Sugar 0.3 g

COFFEE JELLY

Prep Time 5 minutes
Total Time 5 minutes
+ Chilling Time
Servings 4

Ingredients
- 4 tbsp Gelatin
- 1 cup (240 cc) Cold Coffee
- 2 cups (480 cc) Hot Coffee
- 3/4 cup (180 cc) Heavy Cream
- 2 tsp Liquid Stevia

Instructions

Coffee Jelly
1. In a large bowl, soften the gelatin by soaking in the cold coffee for a couple of minutes.
2. Add the hot coffee and stir to dissolve the gelatin.
3. Pour the mixture evenly into 4 glasses. (Or you can pour into a tray and then cut into cubes when set and cold.)
4. Let cool to room temperature. Then refrigerate for 3 hours or until set and cold.

To Serve
1. Optional: Beat the heavy cream and liquid stevia until a bit thick.
2. Make sure that the coffee jelly has set and pour the heavy cream over the jelly.
3. Optional: Soak the crushed jelly in the heavy cream for a while in the fridge before serving.

Recipe Notes:
Adjust the quantity of heavy cream and sweetener to your liking.

Approximate Nutritional Values Per Serving:
No nutrition values for this recipe

STRAWBERRY & YOGURT MOUSSE

Prep Time 20 minutes
Total Time 20 minutes
+ Chilling Time
Servings 6

Ingredients

Yogurt Mousse Layer
- 3 oz (85 g) Cream Cheese, Softened
- 1.5 tsp Stevia Powder
- 3 oz (85 g) Yogurt, Room Temp
- 1 tbsp Lemon Juice
- 1/4 cup (60 cc) Heavy Cream
- 1 tbsp Water
- 2 tsp (6 g) Gelatin
- 2 tbsp Boiling Water

Strawberry Yogurt Mousse Layer
- 3 oz (85 g) Frozen Strawberries, Thawed
- 1 tsp Water
- 1/4 tsp Gelatin
- 1 tsp Boiling Water

Instructions

Yogurt Mousse Layer
1. In a large bowl, beat the cream cheese and stevia together. Add the yogurt and lemon juice and beat well.
2. In another bowl, beat the heavy cream until soft peaks form.
3. Fold in the whipped heavy cream to the yogurt mixture.
4. In a small bowl, soften the gelatin by soaking in the water for a couple of minutes. Add the boiling water and stir well to dissolve the gelatin.
5. Add the gelatin mixture to the yogurt mixture and mix well.
6. Reserve 1/3 of the yogurt mixture in a separate bowl. Set aside.
7. Spoon the remaining yogurt mixture into a 6-cavity silicone mold.
8. Place the mold in the freezer while preparing the strawberry yogurt mousse layer.

Strawberry Yogurt Mousse Layer
1. Crush the strawberries in a medium bowl.
2. Add the strawberries to the reserved yogurt mixture and stir well.
3. In a small bowl, soften the gelatin by soaking in the water for a couple of minutes. Add the boiling water and stir well to dissolve the gelatin.
4. Add the gelatin mixture to the strawberry mixture and mix well.
5. Remove the silicone mold from the freezer.
6. Spoon the strawberry mixture over the yogurt mousse.
7. Refrigerate for 2 hours or until set.
8. Run a toothpick around the edge of each cup and remove the mousse. (* If you still find it difficult to remove the mousse from the mold, freeze for about 20 - 30 minutes and remove, and then store the mousse back in the fridge.)

Approximate Nutritional Values Per Serving:
Calories 106 kcal, Protein 2.0 g, Total Fat 9.6 g, Total Carbohydrate 2.5 g, Dietary Fiber 0.2 g, Sugar 2.3 g

STRAWBERRY-STUFFED NO-BAKE CHOCOLATE CHEESECAKE BITES

Prep Time 15 minutes
Cook Time 1 minute
Total Time 16 minutes
+ Chilling Time
Servings 7 pieces

Ingredients

Chocolate
- 1 oz (28 g) Coconut Oil
- 3 oz (85 g) Unsweetened Baking Chocolate, Chopped
- 1.5 tsp Liquid Stevia
- 2 tsp Vanilla Extract

Chocolate Cheesecake
- 4 oz (112 g) Cream Cheese, Softened
- 2 tsp Stevia Powder
- 2 tsp Vanilla Extract
- 3/4 cup (180 cc) Heavy Cream
- 1/4 cup (0.63 oz / 18 g) Unsweetened Cocoa Powder
- 1 tbsp Water
- 1.5 tsp (0.16 oz / 4.5 g) Gelatin
- 1.5 tbsp Boiling Water
- 7 Small Strawberries (When removing the stems, pull them rather than cutting off the flesh)

Instructions

Chocolate
1. Melt the coconut oil in a saucepan over low heat. Turn off the heat when half melted.
2. Add the unsweetened chocolate. Leave a couple minutes and then stir until

melted. Add the liquid stevia and vanilla, and mix.

3. Place 2 teaspoons of the chocolate into each hole of your Egg Bites Mold. Reserve the rest of the chocolate for later.

4. Chill for 10 minutes.

Chocolate Cheesecake

1. While chilling the chocolate, beat the heavy cream in a large bowl until soft peaks form. Set aside.
2. In another bowl, cream the cream cheese using the same hand mixer. Add the stevia powder and vanilla, and beat until smooth and well-combined.
3. Beat in the cocoa powder and whipped cream.
4. In a small bowl, soften the gelatin by soaking in the water for a couple of minutes. Add the boiling water and stir to dissolve the gelatin.
5. Add the gelatin mixture to the cheesecake mixture. Beat until well combined.

Assembly

1. Remove the egg bites mold from the fridge. Pop the chocolate out of the mold and then replace. (* This process is to make it easier to remove the whole cheesecake bites later.)

2. Place 2 tablespoons of the cheesecake mixture into each hole of the egg bites mold, over the chocolate.
3. Place a strawberry flat side up in the middle of each hole of the egg bites mold. Fill with the remaining cheesecake mixture. Flatten the tops of each.

4. Chill for 30 minutes.
5. Re-melt the reserved chocolate over low heat if necessary. Remove the egg bites mold from the fridge. Place 1 - 1.5 tablespoons of the chocolate over the cheesecake mixture. (* Reserve about 2 tablespoons of the chocolate for drizzling later if desired.)
6. Chill for another 90 - 120 minutes or until set.
7. Remove from the fridge. Run a spatula that came with your egg bites mold around each hole. Clean the spatula whenever necessary. Then invert on a plate. Remove the cheesecake bites carefully.

8. Optional: Drizzle the reserved chocolate over top. Chill for 5 minutes until set.

Approximate Nutritional Values Per Serving:
Calories 257 kcal, Protein 4.5 g, Total Fat 25.9 g, Total Carbohydrate 7.5 g, Dietary Fiber 2.8 g, Sugar 2.8 g

PEANUT BUTTER MASCARPONE JARS

Prep Time 10 minutes
Cook Time 15 minutes
Total Time 25 minutes
+ Chilling Time
Servings 4 or 5 jars

Ingredients

Base
- 1.76 oz (50 g) Almond Flour (About 1/2 cup: Measure by weight if possible)
- 2 tbsp Unsweetened Cocoa Powder
- 1/2 tsp Stevia Powder
- 0.75 oz (21 g) Unsalted Butter, Melted
- 1/2 tsp Vanilla Extract

Filling
- 4 oz (112 g) Mascarpone Cheese, Room Temp
- 1/3 cup (80 g) Creamy Peanut Butter, Room Temp
- 1/2 tbsp Stevia Powder
- 1 tsp Vanilla Extract
- 1/2 cup (120 cc) Heavy Cream
- A Pinch of Sea Salt

Topping (Optional)
- Sugar Free Chocolate Chips, Unsweetened Cocoa Powder, etc

Instructions

Base
1. Preheat the oven to 180 C / 350 F.
2. In a mixing bowl, whisk the almond flour, cocoa and stevia.
3. Add the butter and vanilla. Stir until a soft dough forms.
4. Spread the dough into a 5-inch / 12.5 cm square on a baking sheet lined with parchment paper.
5. Bake for 15 minutes.
6. Let cool completely on a wire rack.
7. When cooled, place in a resealable plastic bag and seal. Crush finely with a rolling pin.
8. Divide among 4 or 5 Mason jars.
9. Set aside.

Filling
1. In a large bowl, beat the mascarpone and peanut butter until creamy. Add the stevia and vanilla and mix well.
2. In a separate bowl, beat the heavy cream and salt until stiff peaks form. Add to the mascarpone mixture and mix well.
3. Place in a piping bag. (* Refrigerate for 20 - 30 minutes if necessary. Depending on the room temperature, it may be too runny for piping.)
4. Pipe into each jar.
5. Refrigerate for 1 - 2 hours.

Topping
1. Optional: Sprinkle the chocolate chips or dust with the cocoa powder, if desired.

Approximate Nutritional Values Per Serving:
- 1/5:
Calories 400 kcal, Protein 8.1 g, Total Fat 38.9 g, Total Carbohydrate 7.2 g, Dietary Fiber 2.6 g, Sugar 2.4 g
- 1/4:
Calories 500 kcal, Protein 10.2 g, Total Fat 48.7 g, Total Carbohydrate 9.0 g, Dietary Fiber 3.3 g, Sugar 3.0 g

PANNA COTTA WITH BERRY JELLY

Prep Time 20 minutes
Total Time 20 minutes
+ Chilling Time
Servings 4

Ingredients

Panna Cotta
- 3/4 cup (180 cc) Heavy Cream
- 2 tsp Stevia Powder
- 1 tsp (3 g) Gelatin
- 1 tbsp Water
- 1/4 cup (60 cc) Heavy Cream

Berry Jelly
- 1 tsp (3 g) Gelatin
- 2 tbsp Water
- 2 tbsp Boiling Water
- 4 oz (112 g) Frozen Berries, Thawed
- 1 tbsp Lemon Juice
- 2 tsp Liquid Stevia

Instructions

Panna Cotta
1. In a small bowl, soften the gelatin by soaking in the water.
2. Place the 3/4 cup heavy cream and stevia into a saucepan over low heat until the sweetener dissolves.
3. Add the gelatin mixture to the saucepan and simmer until the gelatin has dissolved. Remove from the heat.
4. Rest a sieve over the top of a bowl and pour the mixture into the sieve, then chill the bowl in an ice bath (ice cubes + water).
5. While chilling the mixture, beat the 1/4 cup heavy cream until soft peaks form. Add to the mixture and stir well.
6. Pour into 4 glasses and chill for 2 - 3 hours until set.

Berry Jelly
1. In a small bowl, soften the gelatin by soaking in the water for a couple of minutes. Add the boiling water and stir well to dissolve the gelatin.
2. Crush the berries in a medium bowl. Add the gelatin mixture, lemon juice and stevia and mix well.
3. Make sure the panna cotta has set and pour the jelly over the panna cotta.
4. Chill for 2 - 3 hours or until set.

Approximate Nutritional Values Per Serving
When Using Strawberries**:**
Calories 236 kcal, Protein 2.8 g, Total Fat 23.4 g, Total Carbohydrate 4.5 g, Dietary Fiber 0.4 g, Sugar 4.1 g

MAGIC COFFEE MOUSSE

Prep Time 5 minutes
Cook Time 1 minute
Total Time 6 minutes
+ Chilling Time
Servings 3

Ingredients

Coffee Mousse
- 1/2 cup (120 cc) Strong Coffee, Room Temp
- 1/6 cup (40 cc) Heavy Cream
- 1 tsp Liquid Stevia
- 0.2 oz (6 g) Gelatin (About 2 tsp)
- 1/2 cup (120 cc) Heavy Cream
- A Pinch of Sea Salt

Toppings
- 1/4 cup (60 cc) Heavy Cream
- 1/2 tsp Stevia Powder
- 1/2 tsp Vanilla Extract
- 1/4 tsp Unsweetened Cocoa Powder

Instructions

Coffee Mousse
1. In a saucepan, heat the coffee, 1/6 cup heavy cream, and stevia until warm. Remove from the heat. Sprinkle with the gelatin and stir. Set aside to let cool to room temperature.
2. In a mixing bowl, beat the 1/2 cup heavy cream and salt until soft peaks.
3. Add the coffee mixture to the whipped cream in 5 parts. Stir between each addition. (* Do not overmix because overmixing may not let the separation occur. There may be tiny lumps left, but it's okay.)
4. Strain the mixture through a fine sieve evenly into 3 glasses / jars. Using a spoon / spatula, force the tiny lumps through the sieve into each glass / jar.

5. Cover and refrigerate for 4 hours or until set and cold. (* It will separate into 2 layers only a few minutes after straining into the glasses / jars.)

Toppings
1. Beat the heavy cream, stevia powder, and vanilla until stiff peaks form. Place in a piping bag and pipe over the coffee mousse.
2. Dust with the cocoa powder.

Recipe Notes:
This coffee mousse separates into 2 layers on its own: Mousse and Jelly.

Approximate Nutritional Values Per Serving:
Calories 327 kcal, Protein 3.3 g, Total Fat 32.7 g, Total Carbohydrate 2.7 g, Dietary Fiber 0 g, Sugar 2.6 g

MAPLE NUT BRIE

Prep Time 1 minutes
Cook Time 15 minutes
Total Time 16 minutes
Servings 4

Ingredients
- 1 wheel (4.5 oz / 125 g) Brie or Camembert Cheese
- 1 oz (28 g) Toasted Nuts (See the Recipe Notes below)
- 1/3 cup (90 g) Sugar Free Maple Syrup
- A Pinch of Ground Cinnamon (Optional)

Instructions
1. Preheat the oven to 180 C / 350 F.
2. Place the brie or camembert on a cast iron skillet. Bake for 15 minutes.
3. While baking, mix together the nuts and maple syrup.
4. Remove the skillet from the oven. Then, pour the maple syrup over the baked brie. (* Be careful because the syrup may bubble rapidly on the hot skillet.)
5. Optional: Sprinkle the cinnamon on top.
6. Serve hot.

Recipe Notes:
This recipe was newly created for this cookbook. If you don't have toasted nuts, you can bake your nuts with a brie and just pour sugar free maple syrup when baked.

Approximate Nutritional Values Per Serving:
Calories 145 kcal, Protein 6.7 g, Total Fat 12.8 g, Total Carbohydrate 1.1 g, Dietary Fiber 0.4 g, Sugar 0.6 g

LEMON CHEESECAKE SMOOTHIE

Prep Time 3 minutes
Total Time 3 minutes
+ Chilling Time
Servings 2

Ingredients
- 2.5 oz (70 g) Cream Cheese, Room Temp
- 2.5 oz (70 g) Mascarpone Cheese, Room Temp
- 1 cup (240 cc) Unsweetened Almond Milk
- 2 tbsp Lemon Juice
- 1 tsp Liquid Stevia
- 1/2 tsp Vanilla Extract
- 1 tbsp Lemon Zest (From 1 Lemon)

Instructions
1. Mix the cream cheese and mascarpone cheese in a food processor / blender until smooth and creamy.
2. Add the almond milk, lemon juice, stevia, vanilla and 1/2 of the lemon zest. (* Reserve the other 1/2 of the lemon zest for topping.) Blend well.
3. Pour into 2 glasses.
4. Refrigerate 30 - 60 minutes.
5. Sprinkle with the remaining lemon zest.

Approximate Nutritional Values Per Serving:
Calories 299 kcal, Protein 5.4 g, Total Fat 28.7 g, Total Carbohydrate 2.7 g, Dietary Fiber 0 g, Sugar 2.7 g

AVOCADO CHOCOLATE SMOOTHIE

Prep Time 3 minutes
Total Time 3 minutes
Servings 2

Ingredients
- 1 Avocado, Peeled & Pitted
- 3/4 cup (180 cc) Water
- 1/3 cup (80 cc) Heavy Cream
- 3 tbsp Unsweetened Cocoa Powder
- 1 tbsp Almond Butter
- 1 tsp Liquid Stevia
- 2 tsp Vanilla Extract
- 1/2 tsp Ground Cinnamon
- A Pinch of Sea Salt
- 8 to 10 Ice Cubes

Instructions
1. Place all the ingredients except for the ice cubes in a food processor / blender. Blend well until smooth and creamy.
2. Add the ice cubes and blend.
3. Pour into 2 glasses.
4. Optional: Refrigerate 30 - 60 minutes before serving.

Recipe Notes:
This recipe was newly created for this cookbook.
Approximate Nutritional Values Per Serving:
Calories 362 kcal, Protein 6.6 g, Total Fat 36.1 g, Total Carbohydrate 12.5 g, Dietary Fiber 7.7 g, Sugar 4.2 g

SUPER-EASY KETO BREAD

Prep Time 5 minutes
Cook Time 40 minutes
Total Time 45 minutes
Servings 15 slices

Ingredients
- 4 oz (112 g) Cream Cheese
- 3 oz (85 g) Walnuts
- 5 Medium Eggs
- 1 oz (28 g) Almond Flour (1/4 cup: Measure by weight if possible)

Instructions
1. Preheat the oven to 220 C / 425 F.
2. Pulse the cream cheese and walnuts in a food processor.
3. Add the eggs and almond flour to the food processor and process until well combined. (* It's okay even if your walnuts are only coarsely ground. You can enjoy the crumbs when eating.)
4. Pour the batter into an 8 x 4 inch / 20 x 10 cm loaf pan lined with parchment paper.
5. Drop the pan a few times to get the air bubbles out.
6. Bake for about 35 - 40 minutes.

Recipe Notes:
This bread (adopted from a bread recipe which was popular among Japanese low-carbers) has a texture and taste like whole grain bread.

Approximate Nutritional Values Per Serving:
Calories 101 kcal, Protein 3.9 g, Total Fat 9.1 g, Total Carbohydrate 1.3 g, Dietary Fiber 0.6 g, Sugar 0.5 g

CREAM CHEESE DANISH

Prep Time 20 minutes
Cook Time 20 minutes
Total Time 40 minutes
Servings 6

Ingredients

Cream Cheese Filling
- 4 oz (112 g) Cream Cheese, Softened
- 2 tbsp Heavy Cream
- 1 tsp Lemon Juice
- 1/2 tsp Vanilla Extract
- 1/2 tsp Liquid Stevia
- Blueberries (Optional)

Fat Head Dough
- 1 1/2 cups (160 g) Shredded Mozzarella Cheese
- 2 oz (56 g) Cream Cheese
- 1 Egg
- 3 oz (85 g) Almond Flour (OR 4 tbsp (30 g) Coconut Flour)
- 1/2 tsp Stevia Powder
- 1/2 tsp Aluminum-Free Baking Powder
- 1 tsp Xanthan Gum (Optional but helps the texture)

To Dust (Optional)
- 1/2 tsp Powdered Sweetener

Instructions

Cream Cheese Filling
1. Combine all the ingredients except for the blueberries in a food processor until creamy.
2. Set aside.

Fat Head Dough
1. In a large saucepan, melt the mozzarella cheese and cream cheese over low heat until it can be stirred together and remove from the heat. (Or microwave 1 - 1.5 minutes.)
2. Stir until well combined.
3. Add the egg and stir.
4. Add the rest of the dough ingredients and mix well.
5. Wet your hand and knead it until uniform. (* Reheat the dough if it gets crumbly. Add flour little by little (like 1/2 tsp at a time) if the dough is too sticky.)
6. Place the dough on a parchment paper. Cover with another parchment paper and roll it out with a rolling pin.

Assembly (Choose either one of the following 3 shapes.)

A. Diamond
1. Preheat the oven to 200 C / 400 F.
2. Cut the dough into 6 squares.
3. Fold a square in half diagonally. Make 2 diagonal cuts along the outside edge of the triangle. Make sure the cuts do not touch.

4. Unfold the square.
5. Take the outer flap and fold it over towards the opposite side.

6. Repeat on the other side to form a diamond shape.
7. Add the cream cheese filling and blueberries to the center.

8. Repeat with the remaining squares.
9. Bake for 16 - 20 minutes.
10. Optional: Dust with the sweetener.

B. Pinwheel
1. Preheat the oven to 200 C / 400 F.
2. Cut into 6 squares.
3. Make 4 equal cuts at each corner of the square. Do not cut all the way through.

4. Fold each flap towards the center.

5. Place the cream cheese filling and blueberries in the center.
6. Repeat with the remaining squares.
7. Bake for 16 - 20 minutes.
8. Optional: Dust with the sweetener

C. Braid
1. Preheat the oven to 200 C / 400 F.
2. Roll out into a large rectangle.
3. Put the cream cheese filling down the center of dough. Sprinkle the blueberries over the filling.
4. Make even slits on both sides of dough.

5. Fold the flaps of the dough diagonally over the filling.
6. Bake for 18 - 20 minutes.
7. Optional: Dust with the sweetener
8. Cut into 6 slices and serve.

Recipe Notes:
Keep refrigerated. Reheat in a toaster oven / oven for a few minutes before serving.

Approximate Nutritional Values Per Serving:
Calories 298 kcal, Protein 14.3 g, Total Fat 24.8 g, Total Carbohydrate 5.5 g, Dietary Fiber 1.8 g, Sugar 2.0 g

CHEESY COCONUT FLOUR BISCUITS

Prep Time 10 minutes
Cook Time 20 minutes
Total Time 30 minutes
Servings 8 biscuits

Ingredients
- 4 Large Eggs
- 2 oz (56 g) Unsalted Butter, Melted
- 1.5 oz (42 g) Coconut Flour (1/3 cup: Measure by weight if possible)
- 1 tsp Aluminum-Free Baking Powder
- 1 tsp Onion Powder or Garlic Powder, or BOTH
- 1 tsp Dried Parsley
- 1/2 tsp Sea Salt
- 6 oz (170 g) Shredded Mozzarella Cheese

Instructions
1. Preheat the oven to 200 C / 400 F.
2. In a medium bowl, whisk together the eggs and melted butter.
3. In a separate bowl, whisk together the coconut flour, baking powder, onion powder, parsley and salt.
4. Combine well the wet and dry ingredients.
5. Stir in the mozzarella cheese.
6. Place 8 mounds of the dough onto a cooking sheet lined with parchment paper. Do not flatten the mounds.
7. Bake for 16 - 20 minutes or until slightly browned.

Recipe Notes:
Reheat them before serving for a fluffy texture.
Approximate Nutritional Values Per Serving:
Calories 138 kcal, Protein 9.1 g, Total Fat 10.6 g, Total Carbohydrate 0.7 g, Dietary Fiber 0 g, Sugar 0.3 g

CURRY PUFFS

Prep Time 20 minutes
Cook Time 50 minutes
Total Time 1 hour 10 minutes
Servings 6

Ingredients

Filling
- 7 oz (200 g) Ground Beef (or Pork)
- 1/2 tsp Salt
- 1/4 tsp Pepper
- 1.5 tbsp Curry Powder
- 1 tbsp Sugar Free Tomato Ketchup
- 1 cup (240 cc) Vegetable Broth
- 2 oz (56 g) Shredded Mozzarella
- 1 tsp Lard

Fat Head Dough
- 1 1/2 cups (160 g) Shredded Mozzarella Cheese
- 2 oz (56 g) Cream Cheese
- 1 Egg
- 3 oz (85 g) Almond Flour (OR 4 tbsp (30 g) Coconut Flour)
- 1 tsp Aluminum-Free Baking Powder
- 1/2 tsp Xanthan Gum (Optional but helps the texture)

Instructions

Filling
1. In a frying pan, cook the lard over medium high heat.
2. Add the meat and cook until browned.
3. Add the salt, pepper, curry powder and ketchup. Stir well.
4. Add the vegetable broth and simmer for about 20 minutes.
5. Let cool completely.

Fat Head Dough
1. In a large saucepan, melt the mozzarella cheese and cream cheese over low heat until it can be stirred together and remove from the heat. (Or microwave 1 - 1.5 minutes.)
2. Stir until well combined.
3. Add the egg and stir.

4. Add the almond (or coconut) flour, baking powder and xanthan gum and mix well.
5. Wet your hand and knead it until uniform. (* Reheat the dough if it gets crumbly. Add flour little by little (like 1/2 tsp at a time) if the dough is too sticky.)

Recipe Notes:
Reheat in a toaster oven / oven for a few minutes before serving.

Approximate Nutritional Values Per Serving:
Calories 315 kcal, Protein 21.7 g, Total Fat 23.1 g, Total Carbohydrate 5.6 g, Dietary Fiber 2.1 g, Sugar 1.7 g

Assembly
1. Preheat the oven to 180 C / 350 F.
2. Place the dough on a parchment paper. Cover it with another parchment paper and roll it out to a 15 x 12 inch / 40 x 30 cm rectangle.
3. Cut the dough into 6 squares.
4. Place the cooked meat and shredded cheese on each square and fold diagonally to form a triangle. Press the edges together and crimp with a fork. (* Wetting your hands and fork definitely helps.)

5. Bake for 20 - 23 minutes or until golden brown.

CHOCOLATE BABKA

Prep Time 30 minutes
Cook Time 70 minutes
Total Time 1 hour 40 minutes
Servings 10 slices

Ingredients

Chocolate Cream Cheese Filling
- 6 oz (170 g) Cream Cheese, Softened
- 1/3 cup (80 cc) Heavy Cream
- 6 tbsp Cocoa Powder
- 1 tbsp Cinnamon
- 2 tsp Liquid Stevia
- 2 tsp Vanilla Extract
- 5 to 6 tbsp Sugar Free Chocolate Chips (Optional: To Sprinkle over Filling)

Fat Head Dough
- 2 1/2 cups (270 g) Shredded Mozzarella Cheese
- 3 oz (85 g) Cream Cheese
- 2 Eggs
- 1.5 oz (45 g) Coconut Flour (OR 4.5 oz (125 g) Almond Flour)
- 1 tbsp Aluminum-Free Baking Powder
- 1 tsp Stevia Powder
- 1 tsp Xanthan Gum (Optional but helps the texture)
- 1 tsp Vanilla Extract

Instructions

Chocolate Cream Cheese Filling
1. Beat the cream cheese in a large bowl.
2. Add the rest of the filling ingredients except for the chocolate chips and mix well.
3. Set aside.

Fat Head Dough
1. In a large saucepan, melt the mozzarella cheese and cream cheese over low heat until it can be stirred together and remove from the heat. (Or microwave 1 - 1.5 minutes.)
2. Stir until well combined.

3. Add the eggs and stir.
4. Add the rest of the dough ingredients and mix well.
5. Wet your hand and knead the dough until uniform. (* Reheat the dough if it gets crumbly. Add flour little by little (like 1/2 tsp at a time) if the dough is too sticky.)

Assembly
1. Preheat the oven to 190 C / 375 F.
2. Divide the dough into 2 equal portions and place one of the dough on a parchment paper. (* Place the other dough in a warm place. The dough tends to break easily if cold when you work with it later.)
3. Top the dough with another piece of parchment paper and roll out into a 15 x 10 inch / 37.5 x 25 cm rectangle.
4. Spread 1/2 of the chocolate cream cheese filling over the dough, leaving a 1-inch / 2.5 cm border all around.
5. Optional: Sprinkle 1/2 of the chocolate chips over the filling if you want it more chocolatey.
6. Roll the dough up into a log.
7. Cut the dough into half lengthwise.
8. Twist the 2 strands around each other, trying to keep the cut sides facing out. Pinch the ends together.

9. Transfer the dough into a loaf pan by forming a ring and placing the seam side down in the half side of the pan.

10. Repeat with the other dough.
11. Bake for 60 - 70 minutes. (* Cover with aluminum foil halfway through the baking (20 - 25 minutes after).)

12. Allow to cool for 10 - 15 minutes in the pan, and then remove from the pan and let cool completely on a wire rack. (* It's soft when warm. It will harden up as it cools. Also, it rises while baking but shrinks a bit as it cools.)

Recipe Notes:
Reheat in a toaster oven / oven before serving for a soft / fluffy texture.
Also, if you find the interior a bit wet when slicing before serving and you don't like it, just transfer the slices to the toaster oven / oven and bake a few minutes. (* However, with a 60 - 70 minute baking time, it should be baked well.)

Approximate Nutritional Values Per Serving
Sans Sugar Free Chocolate Chips:
Calories 249 kcal, Protein 12.8 g, Total Fat 19.4 g, Total Carbohydrate 6.9 g, Dietary Fiber 2.8 g, Sugar 3.0 g

CINNAMON BABKA WITH CINNAMON GLAZE

Prep Time 30 minutes
Cook Time 70 minutes
Total Time 1 hour 40 minutes
Servings 10 slices

Ingredients

Cream Cheese Filling
- 3 oz (85 g) Cream Cheese, Softened
- 1 tbsp Heavy Cream
- 1.5 tsp Stevia Powder
- 1 tsp Vanilla Extract
- 0.5 oz (14 g) Chopped Walnuts

Cinnamon Filling
- 4 oz (112 g) Unsalted Butter, Softened
- 2 tbsp Ground Cinnamon
- 3/4 tbsp Stevia Powder
- 0.5 oz (14 g) Chopped Walnuts

Fat Head Dough
- 2 1/2 cups (270 g) Shredded Mozzarella Cheese
- 3 oz (85 g) Cream Cheese
- 2 Eggs
- 1.5 oz (45 g) Coconut Flour (4.5 oz (125 g) Almond Flour)
- 1 tbsp Aluminum-Free Baking Powder
- 1 tsp Stevia Powder
- 1 tsp Xanthan Gum (Optional but helps the texture)
- 1 tsp Vanilla Extract

Glaze
- 2/3 cup (90 g) Confectioners Swerve
- 1.5 tsp Ground Cinnamon
- 1/4 cup (60 cc) Water
- 1/2 tsp Vanilla Extract

Instructions

Cream Cheese Filling
1. Beat the cream cheese in a bowl.
2. Add the heavy cream, stevia and vanilla and mix well.
3. Set aside.

Cinnamon Filling
1. Beat the butter in a bowl.
2. Add the cinnamon and stevia and mix well.
3. Set aside.

Fat Head Dough
1. In a large saucepan, melt the mozzarella cheese and cream cheese over low heat until it can be stirred together and remove from the heat. (Or microwave 1 - 1.5 minutes.)
2. Stir until well combined.
3. Add the eggs and stir.
4. Add the rest of the dough ingredients and mix well.
5. Wet your hand and knead the dough until uniform. (* Reheat the dough if it gets crumbly. Add flour little by little (like 1/2 tsp at a time) if the dough is too sticky.)

Assembly
1. Preheat the oven to 190 C / 375 F.
2. Divide the dough into 2 equal portions and place one of the dough on a parchment paper. (* Place the other dough in a warm place. The dough tends to break easily if cold when you work with it later.)
3. Top the dough with another piece of parchment paper and roll out into a 15 x 10 inch / 37.5 x 25 cm rectangle.

4. Spread the cream cheese filling over the dough, leaving a 1-inch (2.5 cm) border all around. Sprinkle the walnuts. Roll the dough up into a log. Set aside.

5. Repeat with the other dough. Spread the cinnamon filling over the dough, leaving a 1-inch (2.5 cm) border all around. Sprinkle the walnuts. Roll the dough up into a log.

6. Twist the 2 logs around each other. Pinch the ends together.

7. Fold the dough lightly and transfer into a loaf pan.

8. Bake for 60 - 70 minutes. (* Cover with aluminum foil halfway through the baking (20 - 25 minutes after).)

9. Allow to cool for 10 - 15 minutes in the pan, and then remove from the pan and let cool completely on a wire rack. (* It's soft when warm. It will harden up as it cools. Also, it rises while baking but shrinks as it cools.)

10. Wait until the babka is cooled to touch. Then spread the glaze on top.

Glaze
1. Blend together all the glaze ingredients until smooth.

Recipe Notes:
Keep refrigerated if you don't finish in one sitting. Reheat in a toaster oven / oven before serving for a soft / fluffy texture.
Also, if you find the interior a bit wet when slicing before serving and you don't like it, just transfer the slices to the toaster oven / oven and bake a few minutes. (* However, with a 60 - 70 minute baking time, it should be baked well.).
Unlike the Chocolate Babka (Page 62 - 63), reheating this Cinnamon Babka gets messy with the glaze spread on top because the glaze melts, so be careful not to reheat too long. If you know beforehand that you don't eat them all in one sitting and want to keep the rest in the fridge, I suggest you make glaze again at the next sitting. If you don't want the cream cheese filling, please double the cinnamon filling ingredients.

Approximate Nutritional Values Per Serving:
Calories 290 kcal, Protein 11.6 g, Total Fat 24.0 g, Total Carbohydrate 15.4 g, Dietary Fiber 1.9 g, Sugar 3.4 g
(Most of the carbs are from Swerve (Erythritol = sugar alcohol). 90 grams of Swerve is used for the glaze, which means 9 grams of carbs per slice are from Swerve, so please subtract that. However, it may be still high for those who count total carbs not net carbs.

FRENCH SAVORY CAKE (CAKE SALE)

Prep Time 10 minutes
Cook Time 45 minutes
Total Time 55 minutes
Servings 10 slices

Ingredients

- 3 Eggs
- 1 oz (28 g) Coconut Oil (or Unsalted Butter), Melted
- 3.5 oz (100 g) Almond Flour (1 cup: Measure by weight if possible)
- 2 tbsp Parmesan Cheese Powder
- 1 tsp Aluminum-Free Baking Powder
- 2/3 tsp Sea Salt
- 1 tbsp Whey Protein Powder
- 1/4 cup (30 g) Shredded Mozzarella Cheese
- 4 slices Ham, Chopped
- 1/2 cup (50 g) Chopped Fresh Broccoli

Instructions

1. Preheat the oven to 180 C / 350 F. Grease an 8 x 4 inch / 20 x 10 cm loaf pan or line with parchment paper.
2. In a large bowl, whisk well the eggs and coconut oil.
3. Add the almond flour, parmesan, baking powder, salt and whey protein to the egg mixture and mix well.
4. Add the mozzarella, ham and broccoli and stir lightly with a spatula.
5. Pour the batter into the loaf pan.
6. Bake for 40 - 45 minutes. (* Insert a wooden skewer and make sure it comes out clean.)
7. Let it cool on a wire rack.

Recipe Notes:

Store them in the fridge. Bring to room temp or reheat in a toaster oven / oven before serving.

Approximate Nutritional Values Per Serving:
Calories 147 kcal, Protein 8.6 g, Total Fat 11.6 g, Total Carbohydrate 3.1 g, Dietary Fiber 1.4 g, Sugar 0.7 g

HAM, CREAM CHEESE & NUTS PULL-APART RING

Prep Time 20 minutes
Cook Time 25 minutes
Total Time 45 minutes
Servings 6

Ingredients

Fat Head Dough
- 1 1/2 cups (160 g) Shredded Mozzarella Cheese
- 2 oz (56 g) Cream Cheese
- 1 Egg
- 3 oz (85 g) Almond Flour (OR 4 tbsp (30 g) Coconut Flour)
- 1/2 tsp Aluminum-Free Baking Powder
- 1 tsp Xanthan Gum (Optional but helps the texture)

Filling
- 4 slices Ham
- 4 oz (112 g) Cream Cheese
- 1 oz (28 g) Chopped Nuts
- 1/4 tsp (or more) Black Pepper

To Sprinkle over Dough (Optional)
- 1/4 tsp Sea Salt

Instructions

1. In a large saucepan, melt the mozzarella cheese and cream cheese over low heat until it can be stirred together and remove from the heat. (Or microwave 1 - 1.5 minutes.)
2. Stir until well combined.
3. Add the egg and stir.
4. Add the almond flour, baking powder, and xanthan gum and mix well.
5. Wet your hand and knead the dough until uniform. (* Reheat the dough if it gets crumbly. Add flour little by little (like 1/2 tsp at a time) if the dough is too sticky.)
6. Preheat the oven to 180 C / 350 F.
7. Place the dough on a parchment paper.
8. Top the dough with another piece of parchment paper and roll it out into a 15 x 12 inch / 40 x 30 cm rectangle.
9. Place the ham on the dough.

10. Spread the cream cheese on the ham.
11. Sprinkle the chopped nuts and black pepper.
12. Roll up the dough.

13. Place the seam side down on the parchment paper and form a ring. Seal the ends together. (* Wetting your hands definitely helps.)
14. Optional: Sprinkle the sea salt over the dough if desired.
15. With kitchen scissors or a knife, cut from outside edge to two-thirds toward the center of the ring at about 2-inch / 5 cm intervals.

16. Place the parchment paper with the dough onto a baking sheet.
17. Bake for 22 - 25 minutes.

Recipe Notes:
Reheat in a toaster oven / oven for a few minutes before serving.

Approximate Nutritional Values Per Serving:
Calories 336 kcal, Protein 17.2 g, Total Fat 28.0 g, Total Carbohydrate 5.7 g, Dietary Fiber 2.1 g, Sugar 2.0 g

CHOCOLATE CINNAMON PULL-APART BREAD

Prep Time 20 minutes
Cook Time 35 minutes
Total Time 55 minutes
Servings 4 - 6

Ingredients

Filling
- 1 oz (28 g) Chopped Walnuts
- 1 tbsp Ground Cinnamon

Chocolate Sauce
- 1/4 cup (60 cc) Heavy Cream
- 1.5 oz (42 g) Unsweetened Baking Chocolate, Chopped
- 1 tsp Liquid Stevia
- 1 tsp Vanilla Extract

Fat Head Dough
- 1 1/2 cups (160 g) Shredded Mozzarella Cheese
- 2 oz (56 g) Cream Cheese
- 1 Egg
- 3 oz (85 g) Almond Flour (OR 4 tbsp (30 g) Coconut Flour)
- 1/2 tsp Stevia Powder
- 1/2 tsp Aluminum-Free Baking Powder
- 1 tsp Vanilla Extract
- 1/2 tsp Xanthan Gum (Optional but helps the texture)

Topping
- 1/2 tsp Unsweetened Cocoa Powder

Instructions

Chocolate Sauce
1. Bring the heavy cream to a simmer in a saucepan over low heat. Remove from the heat.
2. Add the chocolate and stevia. Stir until melted and smooth.
3. Add the vanilla and mix well.

4. Cool to room temperature and place in a piping bag.

Fat Head Dough
1. In a large saucepan, melt the mozzarella cheese and cream cheese over low heat until it can be stirred together and remove from the heat. (Or microwave 1 - 1.5 minutes.)
2. Stir until well combined.
3. Add the egg and stir.
4. Add the rest of the dough ingredients and mix well.
5. Wet your hand and knead the dough until uniform. (* Reheat the dough if it gets crumbly. Add flour little by little (like 1/2 tsp at a time) if the dough is too sticky.)

Assembly
1. Preheat the oven to 180 C / 350 C.
2. Place the dough on a parchment paper.
3. Top the dough with another piece of parchment paper and roll it out into a 15 x 12 inch / 40 x 30 cm rectangle.
4. Cut the dough into 12 rectangles with a pizza cutter.

5. Pipe the chocolate sauce evenly over the dough.
6. Sprinkle the chopped nuts and cinnamon.

7. Tri-fold each rectangle and layer them in an 8 x 4 inch / 20 x 10 cm loaf pan lined with parchment paper.

8. Bake for 30 - 35 minutes. (* Cover the top with aluminum foil halfway through the baking.)
9. Let cool in the pan for 15 minutes.
10. Dust with the cocoa powder.

Recipe Notes:
Keep refrigerated. Reheat in a toaster oven / oven for a few minutes before serving.

Approximate Nutritional Values Per Serving:
- 1/4:
Calories 482 kcal, Protein 21.5 g, Total Fat 41.9 g, Total Carbohydrate 11.3 g, Dietary Fiber 4.7 g, Sugar 2.5 g
- 1/5:
Calories 385 kcal, Protein 17.2 g, Total Fat 33.5 g, Total Carbohydrate 9.0 g, Dietary Fiber 3.7 g, Sugar 2.0 g
- 1/6:
Calories 321 kcal, Protein 14.3 g, Total Fat 27.9 g, Total Carbohydrate 7.5 g, Dietary Fiber 3.1 g, Sugar 1.6 g

PEANUT BUTTER STUFFED SKILLET ROLLS WITH CHOCOLATE DIPPING SAUCE

Prep Time 25 minutes
Cook Time 25 minutes
Total Time 50 minutes
Servings 10 rolls

Ingredients

Peanut Butter Filling
- 6 tbsp Unsweetened Peanut Butter
- 1 tsp Ground Cinnamon (Optional)
- 1/2 tsp Stevia Powder

Fat Head Dough
- 2 1/2 cups (270 g) Shredded Mozzarella Cheese
- 3 oz (85 g) Cream Cheese
- 2 Eggs
- 1.5 oz (45 g) Coconut Flour
- 1 tbsp Aluminum-Free Baking Powder
- 1 tsp Stevia Powder
- 1 tsp Xanthan Gum (Optional but helps the texture)
- 1 tsp Vanilla Extract

Chocolate Dipping Sauce
- 1/3 cup (80 cc) Heavy Cream
- 1.5 oz (45 g) Unsweetened Baking Chocolate, Chopped
- 1 tsp Liquid Stevia
- 1 tsp Vanilla Extract

Instructions

Peanut Butter Filling
1. Mix well all the filling ingredients in a small bowl.
2. Chill in the freezer for about 10 - 15 minutes to make it hard (or use dry / hard peanut butter at the bottom of the jar if any). (* It would be very difficult to

wrap inside the dough if it's too creamy and runny.)

Fat Head Dough
1. In a large saucepan, melt the mozzarella cheese and cream cheese over low heat until it can be stirred together and remove from the heat. (Or microwave 1 - 1.5 minutes.)
2. Stir until well combined.
3. Add the eggs and stir.
4. Add the rest of the dough ingredients and mix well.
5. Wet your hand and knead it until uniform. (* Reheat the dough if it gets crumbly. Add extra coconut flour little by little (like 1/2 tsp at a time) if the dough is too sticky.)

Assembly
1. Preheat the oven to 180 C / 350 F. Butter an 8-inch / 20 cm cast iron skillet.
2. Divide the dough into 10 equal portions. With each of the portions, wrap 1/10 of the peanut butter filling, wetting your hands accordingly. Repeat until you have 10 balls.
3. Arrange the dough balls around the outside of the skillet. (* Place an empty 3.5-inch / 9 cm ramekin in the center if you want.)
4. Bake for about 25 minutes. (* The skillet gets very hot, so be careful when taking it out of the oven.)
5. Let cool for about 10 minutes.

Chocolate Dipping Sauce
1. While cooling the rolls, bring the heavy cream to a simmer in a saucepan over low heat. Remove from the heat.
2. Add the unsweetened chocolate. Stir until melted and smooth.
3. Add the liquid stevia and vanilla and mix well.
4. Pour the sauce into a 3.5-inch / 9 cm ramekin.

To Serve
1. Place the ramekin in the center of the skillet.
2. Dip the rolls into the chocolate sauce and enjoy.

Approximate Nutritional Values Per Serving:
Calories 254 kcal, Protein 13.4 g, Total Fat 19.8 g, Total Carbohydrate 7.4 g, Dietary Fiber 3.0 g, Sugar 2.2 g

CHEESEBURGER STUFFED BAGUETTE

Prep Time 20 minutes
Cook Time 25 minutes
Total Time 45 minutes
Servings 7 slices

Ingredients

Filling
- 7 oz (200 g) Ground Beef
- 1 tbsp Worcestershire Sauce
- 1/4 tsp Salt
- 1/4 tsp Black Pepper
- 1 tsp Lard
- 2 Eggs, Beaten
- 1/2 cup Shredded Cheddar Cheese
- 3 tbsp Ricotta Cheese

Fat Head Dough
- 1 1/2 cups (160 g) Shredded Mozzarella Cheese
- 2 oz (56 g) Cream Cheese
- 3 oz (85 g) Almond Flour (OR 4 tbsp (30 g) Coconut Flour)
- 1 Egg
- 1/2 tsp Aluminum-Free Baking Powder

Topping (Optional)
- 1/2 tsp Chopped Parsley

Instructions

Filling
1. Heat a frying pan on the stove top over medium high and add the lard.
2. Add the beef to the pan. Season with the salt, pepper and Worcestershire sauce. When cooked, set aside to cool.
3. Add the eggs into the pan and scramble. When done, set aside to cool.

Fat Head Dough
1. In a large saucepan, melt the mozzarella cheese and cream cheese over low heat until it can be stirred together and remove from the heat. (Or microwave 1 - 1.5 minutes.)
2. Stir until well combined.
3. Add the egg and stir.
4. Add the almond flour and baking powder and mix well.
5. Wet your hand and knead the dough until uniform. (* Reheat the dough if it gets crumbly. Add flour little by little (like 1/2 tsp at a time) if the dough is too sticky.)

Recipe Notes:
Reheat in a toaster oven / oven before serving.
Approximate Nutritional Values Per Serving:
Calories 304 kcal, Protein 21.2 g, Total Fat 22.5 g, Total Carbohydrate 4.6 g, Dietary Fiber 1.5 g, Sugar 1.3 g

Assembly
1. Preheat the oven to 190 C / 375 F.
2. Place the dough on a parchment paper.
3. Top the dough with another piece of parchment paper and roll it out into a 15 x 12 inch / 40 x 30 cm rectangle.
4. Place the cooled beef and scrambled eggs on the dough, and then spread the cheddar and ricotta.

5. Roll up the dough.
6. Place the seam side down on the parchment paper. Seal both ends.
7. Make diagonal slashes across the top with a sharp knife.

8. Place the parchment paper with the dough onto a baking sheet.
9. Bake for 22 - 25 minutes.
10. Sprinkle the parsley if desired. Cool on a wire rack for 10 - 15 minutes.

HAM & EGG BUNS

Prep Time 25 minutes
Cook Time 23 minutes
Total Time 48 minutes
Servings 4 buns

Ingredients

Egg Mixture
- 2 Hard Boiled Eggs, Chopped
- 2 tbsp Mayonnaise
- 1/2 tsp Whole Grain Mustard
- 1/4 tsp Sea Salt
- A Pinch of Black Pepper

Fat Head Dough
- 1 1/2 cups (160 g) Shredded Mozzarella Cheese
- 2 oz (56 g) Cream Cheese
- 1 Egg
- 3 oz (85 g) Almond Flour (OR 4 tbsp (30 g) Coconut Flour)
- 1 tsp Aluminum-Free Baking Powder
- 1 tsp Xanthan Gum (Optional but helps the texture)

Filling
- 4 slices Ham
- 1 oz (28 g) Shredded Cheddar Cheese

Topping
- 1/2 tsp Chopped Parsley

Instructions

Egg Mixture
1. Mix all the ingredients well.
2. Set aside.

Fat Head Dough
1. In a large saucepan, melt the mozzarella cheese and cream cheese over low heat until it can be stirred together and remove from the heat. (Or microwave 1 - 1.5 minutes.)
2. Stir until well combined.
3. Add the egg and stir.
4. Add the almond flour (or coconut flour), baking powder and xanthan gum and mix well.

5. Wet your hand and knead it until uniform. (* Reheat the dough if it gets crumbly. Add flour little by little (like 1/2 tsp at a time) if the dough is too sticky.)

Assembly
1. Preheat the oven to 180 C / 350 F.
2. Divide the dough into 4 equal portions.
3. Place one portion of the dough on a parchment paper. Cover with another parchment paper and roll it out to a circle slightly (0.5 inch / 1.5 cm) bigger than the prepared ham.
4. Place the ham on the dough. Roll up and place the seam side down. Pinch the ends together to seal. (* Wetting your hands helps.)

5. With a knife, cut the dough lengthwise, leaving about an inch / 2.5 cm intact on the ends.

6. Spread the opening as wide as possible, leaving the bottom layer intact.

7. Place 1/4 of the cheddar cheese, and then 1/4 of the egg mixture into the opening. (* Make sure that the ham on the side is not covered completely by the egg mixture.)
8. Repeat with the remaining 3 portions of the dough.
9. Bake for 20 - 23 minutes.
10. Cool on a wire rack for 10 - 15 minutes.
11. Sprinkle the parsley on top and serve.

Recipe Notes:
Keep refrigerated. Reheat in a toaster oven / oven before serving.

Approximate Nutritional Values Per Serving:
Calories 466 kcal, Protein 27.4 g, Total Fat 36.9 g, Total Carbohydrate 7.4 g, Dietary Fiber 2.5 g, Sugar 2.4 g

GARLIC SHRIMP AVOCADO BREAD

Prep Time 10 minutes
Cook Time 50 minutes
Total Time 1 hour
Servings 10 slices

Ingredients

Garlic Shrimp
- 6 oz (170 g) (10 to 12 count) Peeled & Deveined Shrimp
- 1/2 tbsp Unsalted Butter
- 1 clove Garlic, Minced
- 1/4 tsp Salt
- Black Pepper to Taste

Avocado
- 1 Ripe Avocado, Peeled & Pitted

Bread
- 3.5 oz (100 g) Almond Flour (1 cup: Measure by weight if possible)
- 1 tbsp Coconut Flour
- 2 tbsp Parmesan Cheese Powder
- 1 tsp Aluminum-Free Baking Powder
- 2/3 tsp Sea Salt
- 1/4 tsp Black Pepper
- 3 Medium to Large Eggs
- 0.5 oz (14 g) Coconut Oil (Unsalted Butter), Melted
- 3 tbsp Heavy Cream

Instructions

Garlic Shrimp
1. Place the shrimp in a small bowl. Sprinkle the salt and pepper on the shrimp and mix well with hands.
2. In a frying pan over low heat, melt the butter. Add the garlic.
3. Cook for 1 - 2 minutes and turn the heat to medium. Add the shrimp and cook until pink. (* The shrimp doesn't need to be cooked through as they will be baked in the oven.)
4. Set aside.

Avocado
1. Slice 1/4 of the avocado into 5 pieces. Chop the remaining 3/4 into cubes.

2. Set aside.

Bread
1. Preheat the oven to 180 C / 350 F. Grease an 8 x 4 / 20 x 10 cm loaf pan or line it with parchment paper. (* The pan used for the bread in the pictures is 8.5 x 3.6 inch / 22 x 9 cm.)
2. In a medium bowl, whisk well the almond flour, coconut flour, parmesan, baking powder, sea salt and black pepper.
3. In a large bowl, whisk well the eggs, coconut oil and heavy cream. Add the almond flour mixture and whisk well.
4. Reserving 5 shrimp (count) and avocado slices, add the remaining shrimp (along with the cooked minced garlic) and avocado cubes to the batter and stir lightly with a spatula.

Assembly
1. Pour the batter into the loaf pan and drop the pan a few times.
2. Place the reserved shrimp and avocado slices on top.

3. Bake for about 45 minutes. (* Cover with aluminum foil halfway through the baking if necessary.)
4. Let it cool on a wire rack.

Recipe Notes:
While eating as is is quite tasty, spreading butter over a reheated slice is also good.

Approximate Nutritional Values Per Serving:
Calories 181 kcal, Protein 9.3 g, Total Fat 14.6 g, Total Carbohydrate 4.3 g, Dietary Fiber 2.3 g, Sugar 1.0 g

BERRY TWIST BUNS

Prep Time 30 minutes
Cook Time 23 minutes
Total Time 53 minutes
Servings 10 buns

Ingredients

Fat Head Dough
- 2 1/2 cups (270 g) Shredded Mozzarella Cheese
- 3 oz (85 g) Cream Cheese
- 2 Eggs
- 1.5 oz (43 g) Coconut Flour
- 1 tbsp Aluminum-Free Baking Powder
- 1 tsp Stevia Powder
- 1 tsp Xanthan Gum
- 1 tsp Vanilla Extract

Blueberry Jam Filling
- 4 oz (112 g) Frozen Blueberries, Thawed
- 1 tbsp Lemon Juice
- 1 tsp Stevia Powder
- 1 tsp Chia Seeds
- 1/4 tsp Xanthan Gum

Strawberry Jam Filling
- 5 oz (140 g) Frozen Strawberries, Thawed
- 1 tbsp Lemon Juice
- 1 tsp Stevia Powder
- 1 tsp Chia Seeds
- 1/4 tsp Xanthan Gum

Topping
- 2 oz (56 g) Cream Cheese, Cut into Tiny Cubes

Instructions

Filling
1. Add the blueberries to a saucepan and heat the saucepan over low.
2. Stir well and crush them lightly as they begin to release their juice.
3. Add the lemon juice and stevia and stir.
4. Add the chia seeds and xanthan gum and stir.
5. Remove the saucepan from heat.

6. Let cool completely.
7. Repeat with the strawberries.

Fat Head Dough
1. In a large saucepan, melt the mozzarella cheese and cream cheese over low heat until it can be stirred together and remove from the heat. (Or microwave 1.5 minutes.)
2. Stir until well combined.
3. Add the eggs and stir.
4. Add the rest of the dough ingredients and mix well.
5. Wet your hand and knead the dough until uniform. (* Reheat the dough if it gets crumbly. Add flour little by little (like 1/2 tsp at a time) if the dough is too sticky.)

Assembly
1. Preheat the oven to 180 C / 350 F.
2. Place the dough on a parchment paper.
3. Top the dough with another piece of parchment paper and roll out into a 20 x 12 inch / 50 x 30 cm rectangle.
4. Spread the blueberry filling over one side of the dough and the strawberry filling over the other side of the dough, leaving about 4-inch / 10 cm border on the right and left sides of the dough.

5. Fold one side of the dough towards the center.

6. Repeat with the other side. (* Please make sure that there is about a 2-inch / 5 cm overlap in the center and that the width of the folded dough is at least 7 inch / 17.5 cm long.

7. Cut the dough into 10 strips crosswise with a pizza cutter.

8. Twist each strip and then curl around in a bun shape, tucking the end under, and place on a baking sheet lined with parchment paper. (* Wetting your hands definitely helps.)

9. Sprinkle the cream cheese cubes on top.

10. Bake for 20 - 23 minutes.

Recipe Notes:
Keep refrigerated. Reheat in a toaster oven / oven before serving.
Approximate Nutritional Values Per Serving:
Calories 172 kcal, Protein 11.0 g, Total Fat 11.1 g, Total Carbohydrate 6.9 g, Dietary Fiber 2.2 g, Sugar 3.4 g

SALMON AVOCADO CROQUE CAKE

Prep Time 30 minutes
Cook Time 1 hour 20 minutes
Total Time 1 hour 50 minutes
Servings 7 - 8 slices

Ingredients

Bread
- 3.5 oz (100 g) Almond Flour (1 cup: Measure by weight if possible)
- 1 tsp Aluminum-Free Baking Powder
- 1/2 tsp Xanthan Gum
- 1/4 tsp Stevia Powder
- 1/4 tsp Sea Salt
- 3 Egg Whites
- 2 Eggs
- 1.5 oz (42 g) Unsalted Butter, Melted
- 1 tbsp Heavy Cream

Egg Mixture
- 2 Eggs
- 1/2 cup + 2 tbsp (150 cc) Heavy Cream
- 1/3 tsp Salt
- 1/4 tsp Black Pepper

Filling
- 3.5 oz (100 g) Smoked Salmon
- 1 Avocado, Cut in Half and Then Cut Each Half into 9 Slices
- 7 oz (200 g) Cream Cheese, Cut into Tiny Cubes
- 1/4 cup (30 g) Shredded Mozzarella Cheese

Instructions

Bread
1. Preheat the oven to 180 C / 350 F.
2. In a mixing bowl, whisk well the almond flour, baking powder, xanthan gum, stevia and sea salt.
3. In a large bowl, beat the eggs whites and eggs for 2 minutes at a high speed. Add

the butter and heavy cream and beat to combine. Add the almond flour mixture and mix well.

4. Pour the batter into an 8 x 4 inch / 20 x 10 cm loaf pan lined with parchment paper. (* The pan shown in the pictures is 8.5 x 3.6 inch / 22 x 9 cm.)
5. Bake for 40 - 45 minutes.
6. Let cool on a wire rack.
7. When cooled, cut the bread horizontally into 3 slices, and then remove crusts except the bottom.

Egg Mixture
1. In a mixing bowl, add all the ingredients and whisk well.
2. Transfer to a tray and soak the bread slices for 10 minutes. (* Turn the slices halfway through.)

Assembly
1. Preheat the oven to 200 C / 400 F.
2. Place the bottom slice of bread into the same loaf pan lined with parchment paper. (* If the egg mixture is still left in the tray after soaking, spoon 1/3 of it over the bread slice and then press the slice with the back of a spoon.)
3. Place 1/2 of the smoked salmon over the bread slice. Place 1/2 of the avocado slices over the salmon and then 1/3 of the cream cheese over the salmon.

4. Place another slice of bread over the cream cheese. (* Spoon 1/2 of the remaining egg mixture over the bread slice.) Press the bread slice with the spoon.
5. Place the remaining smoked salmon and avocado slices. Then, place 1/2 of the remaining cream cheese.
6. Place the last slice of bread over the cream cheese. (* Spoon the remaining egg mixture over the bread slice.) Press the bread slice with the spoon.
7. Sprinkle the mozzarella cheese on top and then the remaining cream cheese.
8. Bake for 35 - 40 minutes. (* Cover with aluminum foil halfway through the baking.)
9. Let cool in the pan for 10 minutes. Then, remove from the pan and cool with parchment paper on on a wire rack. When cooled to touch, slice and serve.

Recipe Notes:
Keep refrigerated. Reheat in a toaster oven / oven for a few minutes before serving or let sit and bring to room temp.

Approximate Nutritional Values Per Serving (Including Removed Crusts)**:**
- 1/7:
Calories 464 kcal, Protein 16.5 g, Total Fat 41.5 g, Total Carbohydrate 6.5 g, Dietary Fiber 2.9 g, Sugar 2.3 g
- 1/8:
Calories 406 kcal, Protein 14.3 g, Total Fat 36.3 g, Total Carbohydrate 5.7 g, Dietary Fiber 2.5 g, Sugar 2.0 g

ZUCCHINI & HAM PASTRY ROSES

Prep Time 25 minutes
Cook Time 25 minutes
Total Time 50 minutes
Servings 8 roses

Ingredients

Fat Head Dough
- 1 1/2 cups (160 g) Shredded Mozzarella Cheese
- 2 oz (56 g) Cream Cheese
- 1 Egg
- 3 oz (85 g) Almond Flour (OR 4 tbsp (30 g) Coconut Flour)
- 1/2 tsp Aluminum-Free Baking Powder
- 1/2 tsp Xanthan Gum

Filling
- 4 inch (10 cm) long Zucchini (Diameter: 2 inch / 5 cm or less)
- 8 slices Ham
- 4 tbsp Mayonnaise
- 1/2 tsp Black Pepper

Instructions

Filling
1. Cut the zucchini very very thinly into 40 slices.
2. Cut the ham in half.

Fat Head Dough
1. In a large saucepan, melt the mozzarella cheese and cream cheese over low heat until it can be stirred together and remove from the heat. (Or microwave 1 - 1.5 minutes.)
2. Stir until well combined.
3. Add the egg and stir.
4. Add the almond flour, baking powder and xanthan gum and mix well.
5. Wet your hand and knead it until uniform. (* Reheat the dough if it gets crumbly. Add flour little by little (like 1/2 tsp at a time) if the dough is too sticky.)

Assembly
1. Preheat the oven to 180 C / 350 F.
2. Place the dough on a parchment paper. Cover it with another parchment paper and roll it out to a 15 x 12 inch / 37 x 30 cm rectangle.
3. Stamp out 36 circles using a 2-inch / 5 cm round cookie cutter. Re-roll the trimmings to stamp out 12 more circles (48 circles in total).
4. Lay 6 circles in a line with a small amount of overlap.
5. Spread the mayo over the circles, then sprinkle the black pepper.

6. Lay 5 zucchini slices over the circles with a small amount of overlap, and then 2 half slices of ham over the zucchini.

7. Starting on one end, roll them to the other end.

8. Place in a muffin tin.
9. Continue with the other pieces until you have 8 roses.
10. Bake for about 25 minutes, until golden brown.

Approximate Nutritional Values Per Serving:
Calories 253 kcal, Protein 13.2 g, Total Fat 20.8 g, Total Carbohydrate 4.6 g, Dietary Fiber 1.6 g, Sugar 1.8 g

CHOCOLATE CREAM HORNS

Prep Time 30 minutes
Cook Time 18 minutes
Total Time 48 minutes
Servings 6 cream horns

Ingredients

Fat Head Dough
- 1 1/2 cups (160 g) Shredded Mozzarella Cheese
- 2 oz (56 g) Cream Cheese
- 1 Egg
- 3 oz (85 g) Almond Flour (OR 4 tbsp (30 g) Coconut Flour)
- 1/2 tsp Stevia Powder
- 1/2 tsp Aluminum-Free Baking Powder
- 1/2 tsp Vanilla Extract
- 1 tsp Xanthan Gum (Optional but helps the texture)

Chocolate Cream Cheese Filling
- 6 oz (170 g) Cream Cheese
- 4 tbsp Heavy Cream
- 6 tbsp Cocoa Powder
- 2 tsp Liquid Stevia
- 2 tsp Vanilla Extract
- 1 tsp Cocoa Powder (Optional: To Dust)

Instructions

Fat Head Dough
1. In a large saucepan, melt the mozzarella cheese and cream cheese over low heat until it can be stirred together and remove from the heat. (Or microwave 1 - 1.5 minutes.)
2. Stir until well combined.
3. Add the egg and stir.
4. Add the rest of the dough ingredients and mix well.
5. Wet your hand and knead the dough until uniform. (* Reheat the dough if it gets crumbly. Add flour little by little

(like 1/2 tsp at a time) if the dough is too sticky.)
6. Preheat the oven to 200 C / 400 F.
7. Divide the dough into 6 equal portions.
8. Roll each portion into a long thin piece.
9. Wrap the dough around a cream horn mold.

10. Bake for 16 - 18 minutes.
11. Let cool on a wire rack and remove the molds.

Chocolate Cream Cheese Filling
1. Add all the ingredients to a food processor / blender and blend until creamy.
2. Place into a piping bag.

Assembly
1. Pipe the chocolate cream cheese filling into each horn.
2. Optional: Dust the cream horns with the cocoa powder.

Approximate Nutritional Values Per Serving:
Calories 355 kcal, Protein 16.2 g, Total Fat 30.2 g, Total Carbohydrate 7.8 g, Dietary Fiber 3.1 g, Sugar 3.0 g

Make Your Own Cream Horn Molds:
You can easily make your own molds with a piece of paper and parchment paper. You can also reuse them just by replacing parchment paper.

1. Fold a piece of paper and cut along the folded lines.

2. Roll each square to make a cone shape.

3. Secure the cone with a stapler.

4. Wrap each cone with parchment paper.

BACON PAIN d'EPI

Prep Time 10 minutes
Cook Time 20 minutes
Total Time 30 minutes
Servings 3

Ingredients

Fat Head Dough
- 1 1/2 cups (160 g) Shredded Mozzarella Cheese
- 2 oz (56 g) Cream Cheese
- 1 Egg
- 3 oz (85 g) Almond Flour (OR 4 tbsp (30 g) Coconut Flour)
- 1/2 tsp Aluminum-Free Baking Powder

Filling
- 3 slices Bacon
- 3 Asparagus
- 1/2 tsp Black Pepper

Topping (Optional)
- 1/2 tsp Chopped Parsley

Instructions

Fat Head Dough
1. In a large saucepan, melt the mozzarella cheese and cream cheese over low heat until it can be stirred together and remove from the heat. (Or microwave 1 - 1.5 minutes.)
2. Stir until well combined.
3. Add the egg and stir.
4. Add the almond flour and baking powder and mix well.
5. Wet your hand and knead it until uniform. (* Reheat the dough if it gets crumbly. Add flour little by little (like 1/2 tsp at a time) if the dough is too sticky.)

Assembly
1. Preheat the oven to 180 C / 350 F.
2. Place the dough on a parchment paper. Cover it with another parchment paper and roll it out to a 15 x 12 inch / 40 x 30 cm rectangle.
3. Cut the dough into 3 pieces.

4. Place the bacon and asparagus on each piece and sprinkle the black pepper.

5. Roll up each dough and place the seam side down on the parchment paper.
6. Using a pair of clean kitchen scissors, cut straight into the dough at a 45-degree angle, cutting all the way through the bacon and asparagus, but not all the way through the dough, and move the dough leaflet to one side. Move 2 inch / 5 cm up the roll and repeat, placing the dough leaflet on the alternating side. Repeat all the steps with the other pieces.

7. Bake for about 20 minutes.
8. Sprinkle the parsley on top.

Recipe Notes:
Reheat in a toaster oven / oven before serving.
Approximate Nutritional Values Per Serving:
Calories 505 kcal, Protein 28.4 g, Total Fat 40.6 g, Total Carbohydrate 9.8 g, Dietary Fiber 3.8 g, Sugar 2.7 g

CHEESY WEAVE

Prep Time 15 minutes
Cook Time 25 minutes
Total Time 40 minutes
Servings 4

Ingredients

Fat Head Dough
- 1 1/2 cups (160 g) Shredded Mozzarella Cheese
- 2 oz (56 g) Cream Cheese
- 1 Egg
- 3 oz (85 g) cup Almond Flour (OR 4 tbsp (30 g) Coconut Flour)
- 1/2 tsp Aluminum-Free Baking Powder
- 1 tsp Xanthan Gum (Optional but helps the texture)

Filling
- 2 oz (56 g) Sausage, Cooked and Cut into Thin Slices
- 1 oz (28 g) Nuts, Chopped
- 1/2 cup (55 g) Shredded Mozzarella Cheese
- 2 to 3 tbsp Mayonnaise

Instructions

1. In a large saucepan, melt the mozzarella cheese and cream cheese over low heat until it can be stirred together and remove from the heat. (Or microwave 1 - 1.5 minutes.)
2. Stir until well combined.
3. Add the egg and stir.
4. Add the almond flour, baking powder and xanthan gum and mix well.
5. Wet your hand and knead it until uniform. (* Reheat the dough if it gets crumbly. Add flour little by little (like 1/2 tsp at a time) if the dough is too sticky.)
6. Preheat the oven to 190 C / 375 F.
7. Place the dough on a parchment paper. Cover it with another parchment paper and roll it out to a 15 x 12 inch / 40 x 30 cm rectangle.
8. Cut the dough into half.

9. Place the sausage, nuts, mozzarella cheese and then mayo on one of the dough. Cover with the other half of the dough.

10. Seal the seams.
11. Cut the dough into 8 pieces and weave them. (* It may get messy, but it'll look good once baked.)

12. Bake for 22 - 25 minutes.

Recipe Notes:
Reheat in a toaster oven / oven before serving.
Approximate Nutritional Values Per Serving:
Calories 508 kcal, Protein 25.8 g, Total Fat 42.4 g, Total Carbohydrate 8.8 g, Dietary Fiber 3.1 g, Sugar 3.0 g

SOUFFLE QUICHE

Prep Time 25 minutes
Cook Time 55 minutes
Total Time 1 hour 20 minutes
Servings 6

Ingredients

Crust
- 7 oz (200 g) Almond Flour (2 cups: Measure by weight if possible)
- 1/4 tsp Salt
- 2.5 oz (70 g) Unsalted Butter, Melted

Filling
- 10.5 oz (300 g) Diced Chicken (Thigh or Breast)
- 3 oz (85 g) Chopped Fresh Broccoli (About 1 cup)
- 1 tsp Salt
- 1/4 tsp Black Pepper
- 1 tbsp Coconut Oil or Butter

Sauce
- 4 tbsp Parmesan Cheese Powder
- 3 Eggs, Separated
- 1/2 cup (120 cc) Heavy Cream
- 1/2 cup (55 g) Shredded Mozzarella Cheese
- 3 tbsp Mayonnaise
- 1 tsp Salt
- 1/4 tsp Black Pepper

Topping
- 1/2 tsp Parsley

Instructions

Crust
1. Preheat the oven to 180 C / 350 F. Grease well an 9-inch / 22 cm tart pan and transfer to the fridge.
2. Combine all the ingredients in a bowl. Mix well until a soft dough forms.
3. Press evenly into the bottom and up the sides of the cooled tart pan.
4. Prick all over with a fork.
5. Bake for about 12 minutes.
6. Let cool.

Filling
1. Melt the coconut oil or butter in a frying pan on the stove top over medium - high heat.
2. Add the chicken into the pan. When almost cooked, add the broccoli and season with the salt and black pepper.
3. When cooked, set aside to cool.

Assembly
1. Preheat the oven to 180 C / 350 F.
2. Sprinkle the parmesan cheese powder over the bottom of the crust.
3. Spread the filling evenly over the crust.
4. In a large bowl, beat the egg whites and a pinch of salt until stiff peaks form. (* A little bit of over-whipping is totally fine.)
5. In a separate bowl, whisk well the egg yolks, heavy cream, mayonnaise, salt and black pepper.
6. Fold the egg whites into the egg yolk mixture in 3 additions. (* It's definitely okay to have lumps left if any.)
7. Quickly pour 1/3 of the sauce over the filling.
8. Spread the shredded mozzarella cheese evenly over the sauce.
9. Pour the remaining sauce on top.
10. Bake for about 35 - 40 minutes until golden brown.
11. Sprinkle the parsley on top and serve.

Recipe Notes:
If you want to go nut free, here's a crust recipe using coconut flour:
- 2.82 oz (80 g) Coconut Flour
- 1/4 tsp Salt
- 2 Eggs
- 2.5 oz (70 g) Coconut Oil, Melted

Approximate Nutritional Values Per Serving
When Using Chicken Thigh with Skin**:**
- 1/6:
  Calories 647 kcal, Protein 27.3 g, Total Fat 56.2 g, Total Carbohydrate 7.7 g, Dietary Fiber 4.7 g, Sugar 2.7 g
- 1/8:
  Calories 485 kcal, Protein 20.5 g, Total Fat 42.1 g, Total Carbohydrate 10.3 g, Dietary Fiber 3.5 g, Sugar 2.1 g

BACON & CHEESE WRAPPED PORK BELLY

Prep Time 10 minutes
Cook Time 45 minutes
Total Time 55 minutes
Servings 6 slices

Ingredients
- 10.5 oz (300 g) Pork Belly (Approx Size: 7 x 2.5 inch / 18 x 6.5 cm)
- 1 tsp Coarse Salt
- 1/2 tsp Black Pepper
- 1 tsp Lard
- 8 slices Bacon
- 6 oz (170 g) Cream Cheese, Room Temp
- 2/3 cup (2 oz / 56 g) Shredded Red Cheddar Cheese

Instructions
1. Rub the salt and pepper on the pork belly.
2. Cook the lard in a frying pan or cast iron skillet over medium heat. Brown the pork belly on all sides.
3. Preheat the oven to 200 C / 400 F.
4. Lay 6 slices of bacon vertically on a cutting board, overlapping each slice a little bit. Then lay one slice horizontally on left side of the 6 slices, then one slice on the right side, overlapping each slice a little bit.

5. Spread the cream cheese on the vertically laid bacon slices. Sprinkle the red cheddar on top.
6. Wrap the pork belly with the bacon slices. (* Start from the horizontal ones.)

7. Place the bacon wrapped pork belly on a baking sheet with the seam side down.
8. Bake for about 40 minutes.

Recipe Notes:
Adjust the ingredients according to the size of your pork belly.

Approximate Nutritional Values Per Serving:
Calories 462 kcal, Protein 14.8 g, Total Fat 42.9 g, Total Carbohydrate 0.8 g, Dietary Fiber 0 g, Sugar 0.8 g
(As you can see, the calories and fat are pretty high. Please be aware that an enormous amount of fat / juice is discarded while baking but these values are not subtracted.)

CURRIED EGG ZUCCHINI BOATS

Prep Time 10 minutes
Cook Time 40 minutes
Total Time 50 minutes
Servings 3

Ingredients

- 3 Medium Zucchini (7.8 inch / 20 cm), Cut in Half Lengthwise
- 1/3 cup (75 g) Mayonnaise
- 1 tbsp + 1 tsp Curry Powder
- 1/2 tsp Onion Powder
- 1/2 tsp Garlic Powder
- 1/2 tsp Black Pepper
- 1 tsp Whole Grain Dijon Mustard
- 4 Hard Boiled Eggs, Coarsely Chopped
- 1 1/2 cups (160 g) Shredded Mozzarella Cheese
- 4 slices Crispy Bacon, Chopped into Small Pieces

Instructions

1. Preheat the oven to 180 C / 350 F.
2. Trim ends from the zucchini. Score at about 1/2-inch / 1.2 cm intervals and scoop out insides into a bowl, leaving 1/4 inch / 0.7 cm thick shells. Add the chopped hard boiled eggs to that bowl.
3. In a small bowl, mix well the mayonnaise, curry powder, onion powder, garlic powder, black pepper and mustard. Add to the egg mixture and stir well.
4. Place the zucchini boats in a greased dish or on a baking sheet.
5. Fill each zucchini boat with 1/6 of the curried egg mixture and top with mozzarella cheese.
6. Bake for 30 - 40 minutes, or until the zucchini are tender and the cheese is golden.
7. Top with the bacon pieces.

Approximate Nutritional Values Per Serving:
Calories 566 kcal, Protein 29.2 g, Total Fat 45.9 g, Total Carbohydrate 8.5g, Dietary Fiber 2.5 g, Sugar 4.9 g

PORK BURGER WRAPPED OKRA

Prep Time 10 minutes
Cook Time 15 minutes
Total Time 25 minutes
Servings 3

Ingredients
- 1 pound (450 g) Ground Pork
- 1 tsp Salt
- 1/2 tsp Black Pepper
- 2 tbsp Gluten Free Soy Sauce (or Coconut Aminos)
- 1 tsp Ginger Powder
- 6 pods Okra
- 2 tsp Lard

Sauce
- 2 tsp Gluten Free Soy Sauce (or Coconut Aminos)

Instructions
1. Rinse the okra. Remove skin around top with calyx. Trim off the tip of the stem.
2. In a large bowl, combine the ground pork, salt, pepper, ginger powder and soy sauce. Knead the mixture until uniform. Divide the mixture into 6 equal portions. With each of the portions, wrap one pod of okra.
3. Cook the lard in a frying pan over medium heat. Add the burger wrapped okra. Cook all sides until golden brown. Cook with a lid on until cooked through.
4. Turn off the heat. Remove the burger wrapped okra from the pan.
5. To the grease left on the pan, add the soy sauce for the sauce and mix well. Pour it over the burger wrapped okra.

Approximate Nutritional Values Per Serving:
Calories 382 kcal, Protein 29.7 g, Total Fat 26.0 g, Total Carbohydrate 3.1 g, Dietary Fiber 1.0 g, Sugar 2.1 g

EGG, BACON & CHEESE STUFFED MEATLOAF

Prep Time 15 minutes
Cook Time 50 minutes
Total Time 1 hour 5 minutes
Servings 8 slices

Ingredients

Meat Mixture
- 1 pound (450 g) Ground Pork
- 1 Egg
- 1/2 cup (50 g) Almond Flour
- 1 tbsp Worcestershire Sauce
- 1/2 tsp Garlic Powder
- 1/2 tsp Onion Powder
- 1/2 tsp Parsley
- 1 tsp Sea Salt
- 1/2 tsp Black Pepper

Stuffing
- 4 oz (112 g) Cream Cheese, Softened
- 1/2 cup (55 g) Shredded Mozzarella Cheese
- 4 Hard Boiled Eggs
- 2 slices Cooked Bacon
- 1.5 oz (42 g) Fresh Chopped Broccoli (About 1/2 cup)

Instructions

1. Preheat the oven to 180 C / 350 F.
2. In a large bowl, mix well all the ingredients for the meat mixture with your hand until combined.
3. In an 8 x 4 inch / 20 x 10 cm loaf pan lined with parchment paper, put 3/4 of the meat mixture into the bottom and up the sides, making a trench. Reserve the remaining 1/4 of the meat mixture.
4. Spread 1/2 of the cream cheese over the bottom. Sprinkle 1/2 of the shredded cheese over the cream cheese.

5. Lay the hard boiled eggs over the cheese and cut into 3 slices crosswise.

6. Add the bacon into each one of the slices.

7. Stuff the broccoli into any room available.

8. Sprinkle the remaining shredded cheese. Spread the remaining cream cheese over it.
9. Cover completely with the reserved meat mixture.
10. Bake for 45 - 50 minutes. (* After 40 minutes, remove from the oven, sprinkle more shredded cheese on top and bake 5 - 10 more minutes if desired.)

Recipe Notes:
When slicing, aim for the centerline of each egg.
Approximate Nutritional Values Per Serving:
Calories 303 kcal, Protein 19.8 g, Total Fat 22.9 g, Total Carbohydrate 2.9 g, Dietary Fiber 1.0 g, Sugar 1.3 g

CHICKEN CRUST HAM & BROCCOLI PIE

Prep Time 15 minutes
Cook Time 45 minutes
Total Time 1 hour
Servings 6

Ingredients

Chicken Crust
- 1 lbs (450 g) Ground Chicken
- 1 Egg
- 1 oz (28 g) Grated Parmesan Cheese (About 1/3 cup)
- 1/2 tsp Salt
- 1/4 tsp Garlic Powder

Filling
- 3 oz (85 g) Cream Cheese, Softened
- 1 tbsp Grated Parmesan Cheese
- 1 tbsp Mayonnaise
- 1/3 cup (80 cc) Heavy Cream
- 1/4 tsp Salt
- 1/4 tsp Black Pepper
- 4 slices Ham, Chopped (About 1.76 oz / 50 g)
- 2 oz (56 g) Chopped Fresh Broccoli (Use stem too) (About 1/2 cup)
- 3 oz (85 g) Shredded Mozzarella Cheese

Instructions

1. Preheat the oven to 200 C / 400 F.
2. In a medium bowl, combine all the crust ingredients. Knead until well combined.
3. Reserve 1/3 cup of the mixture and transfer the rest to a 9-inch / 22 cm pie dish.
4. Press evenly into the bottom and up the sides of the pie dish.
5. Bake for about 15 minutes.
6. While baking, cream the cream cheese in a mixing bowl using a spatula.
7. Add the parmesan, mayo, heavy cream, salt and black pepper and stir until combined.
8. Add the ham, broccoli and 1/3 of the mozzarella and stir.

9. Transfer the mixture over the baked chicken crust. (* There will be juice from the chicken on the crust. Leaving there or discarding is up to you.)
10. Place the reserved chicken crust mixture over the filling.

11. Sprinkle the remaining mozzarella cheese.
12. Bake for 25 - 30 minutes.
13. Serve hot.

Approximate Nutritional Values Per Serving:
Calories 293 kcal, Protein 26.7 g, Total Fat 19.0 g, Total Carbohydrate 1.6 g, Dietary Fiber 0.4 g, Sugar 0.9 g

PAN-FRIED BACON WRAPPED ZUCCHINI SKEWERS

Prep Time 15 minutes
Cook Time 10 minutes
Total Time 25 minutes
Servings 4

Ingredients
- 12 slices Bacon
- 1 tsp Salt
- 1/2 tsp Black Pepper
- 1 Zucchini (8 inch / 20 cm long)
- 12 Cherry Tomatoes
- 1/2 Avocado
- 1 tsp Lard (or Other Oil of Choice)

Sauce
- 3 tbsp Gluten Free Soy Sauce (or Coconut Aminos)
- 1 tsp Ground Ginger
- 1 tsp Paprika
- 3 to 4 drops Stevia Liquid

Instructions
1. Mix together the sauce ingredients. Set aside.
2. Cut the bacon slices in half. Sprinkle both sides with the salt and black pepper
3. Cut off each end of the zucchini and cut in thirds. Then cut each third lengthwise into half and then cut each half in half again, ending up with 24 pieces.
4. Cut the avocado into 12 cubes.
5. Wrap each zucchini piece with a bacon strip.
6. Thread a bacon wrapped zucchini onto a skewer. Add a cherry tomato, another bacon wrapped zucchini and then an avocado cube. Repeat with the remaining zucchini pieces, tomatoes and avocado cubes.
7. Cook 1/2 of the lard in a frying pan over medium heat and add 1/2 of the skewers.
8. Pan fry with a lid on until the bacon has turned brown and crisp, about 10 minutes.
9. Turn to low heat. Pour 1/2 of the sauce into the pan and turn the skewers to coat.
10. Repeat with the rest of the skewers.

Recipe Notes:
The recipe yields 12 skewers.
Approximate Nutritional Values Per Serving (3 Skewers)**:**
Calories 308 kcal, Protein 9.3 g, Total Fat 28.5 g, Total Carbohydrate 4.9 g, Dietary Fiber 1.9 g, Sugar 3.0 g

CHEESY AVOCADO STUFFED CHICKEN BURGERS

Prep Time 15 minutes
Cook Time 15 minutes
Total Time 30 minutes
Servings 4

Ingredients

Patties
- 1 pound (450 g) Ground Chicken
- 2 tbsp Grated Parmesan
- 1 tsp Simply Organic's All Purpose Seasoning (or Italian Seasoning)
- 1/2 tsp Sea Salt
- 1/2 tsp Pepper

Avocado Filling
- 1 Small Avocado, Chopped
- 1 tsp Lemon Juice
- 1 tbsp Grated Parmesan Cheese
- 1/4 tsp Sea Salt
- 1/8 tsp Pepper
- 1.5 oz (42 g) Shredded Mozzarella Cheese

Sauce
- 1/4 cup (60 cc) Heavy Cream
- 1/4 cup (60 cc) Chicken Broth (or Vegetable Broth)
- 1 tbsp Grated Parmesan
- 1 oz (28 g) Shredded Mozzarella Cheese
- 1/8 tsp Sea Salt
- 1/8 tsp Pepper

To Cook
- 1 tsp Lard or Avocado Oil

Instructions

1. In a medium bowl, mix together the avocado, lemon juice, parmesan, salt and pepper, mashing the avocado. Add the mozzarella and mix well. Set aside.
2. In a large bowl, thoroughly mix the chicken with the parmesan, seasoning, salt and pepper. Knead until uniform. Divide the mixture into 4 equal portions.

Take 2/3 of one of the portions and form it into a circle about 3 inch / 7.5 cm wide. Put 1/4 of the avocado mixture on it, and then put the remaining of that portion of the chicken mixture onto the top. Pinch around the edge to join the top to the base.

3. Repeat until you have 4 patties.
4. Cook the lard in a frying pan over medium heat. Add the patties and cook side one until golden brown. Turn over and cook with a lid on for about 10 minutes until cooked through.
5. Remove the patties from the pan.
6. In the same pan over low heat, add all the sauce ingredients and stir until creamy.
7. Place the patties back into the pan and simmer for a couple of minutes.
8. Serve immediately.

Recipe Notes:
If you want your sauce to be thicker, please adjust simply by adding more cream or cheese.
Also, if you want more sauce, double the sauce ingredients.

Approximate Nutritional Values Per Serving:
Calories 446 kcal, Protein 36.2 g, Total Fat 31.1 g, Total Carbohydrate 3.9 g, Dietary Fiber 2.1 g, Sugar 1.4 g

DAIKON RADISH POTSTICKERS (JAPANESE GYOZA)

Prep Time 15 minutes
Cook Time 20 minutes
Total Time 35 minutes
Servings 2

Ingredients

Wrappers
- 3 inches (7.5 cm) long Daikon Radish, Peeled (Diameter: About 3 inch / 7.5 cm)
- 2 tsp Salt

Filling
- 9 oz (255 g) Ground Pork
- 3 oz (85 g) Cabbage, Finely Chopped
- 2 tsp Grated Ginger (OR 1 tsp Grated Ginger + 1 tsp Grated Garlic)
- 1 tsp Gluten Free Soy Sauce (or Coconut Aminos)
- 1/2 tsp Salt
- 1/2 tsp Black Pepper
- 2 tbsp Sesame Oil (For Frying)

Dipping Sauce
- 3 tbsp Gluten Free Soy Sauce (or Coconut Aminos)
- 2 tsp Apple Cider Vinegar

Instructions

1. Slice the daikon radish as thinly as possible, using a cabbage slicer.
2. Salt the daikon slices in a tray and let stand 10 minutes until softer.
3. Rinse the daikon slices. Pat them dry with paper towels. Set aside.
4. In a mixing bowl, combine the ground pork, cabbage, ginger, soy sauce, salt, and black pepper. Knead the mixture by hand until uniform.
5. Place about 1.5 teaspoons of the meat mixture on one slice of daikon and fold in half. Press lightly so that the daikon

slice will stick to the filling. Repeat for the rest of the daikon slices.

6. Add 1/2 of the sesame oil to a frying pan over high heat. (* Probably 2 rounds of pan frying will be needed, so only 1/2 is added here.) Place 1/2 of the potstickers on the pan, then turn the heat to medium. Cook until the bottom becomes golden brown. Turn over and cook with a lid on over low heat for 3 - 5 minutes until cooked through. Repeat with the remaining potstickers.
7. Mix together the soy sauce and apple cider vinegar for dipping sauce.

Recipe Notes:
This is a very popular way of eating potstickers among low-carbers in Japan.
You need to slice your daikon radish as thinly as possible, then salt the slices and let stand for 10 minutes until they get softer. By following all this, the daikon radish slices won't crack when folding in half and they will stick to the filling without using potato starch which is usually called for almost all of the daikon radish potsticker recipes.

Approximate Nutritional Values Per Serving:
Calories 448 kcal, Protein 26.5 g, Total Fat 32.4 g, Total Carbohydrate 9.2 g, Dietary Fiber 2.3 g, Sugar 6.8 g

BACON WRAPPED BROCCOLI STUFFED PORK CHOPS

Prep Time 15 minutes
Cook Time 40 minutes
Total Time 55 minutes
Servings 2

Ingredients
- 2 slices Thin Cut Pork Chops (About 9 oz / 250 g)
- 1/2 tsp Salt
- 1/4 tsp Black Pepper
- 6 slices Bacon

Filling
- 2 oz (56 g) Fresh Broccoli, Chopped
- 2 oz (56 g) Cream Cheese, Softened
- 1/4 tsp Salt
- 1/8 tsp Black Pepper
- 1/2 tsp Garlic Powder
- 1/2 tsp Simply Organic's All Purpose Seasoning (or Italian Seasoning)
- 1.5 oz (42 g) Shredded Mozzarella Cheese

Instructions
1. Preheat the oven to 200 C / 400 F.
2. Place the broccoli in a food processor and process. Add the cream cheese, salt, black pepper, garlic powder and seasoning and blend well. Set aside.
3. Flatten the pork chops with a mallet.
4. Sprinkle both sides of each pork chop with the salt and black pepper.
5. Spread the broccoli mixture over each pork chop. Sprinkle the mozzarella over the broccoli mixture.
6. Roll up the pork chops.

7. Lay 3 slices of bacon vertically, overlapping each slice a little bit. Place one of the rolled pork chops at one end of the bacon and roll up. Repeat with the other pork chop.

8. Place on a baking sheet with the seam side down.
9. Bake for about 40 minutes.
10. Serve as is or with your favorite sauce.

Approximate Nutritional Values Per Serving:
Calories 728 kcal, Protein 39.2 g, Total Fat 60.5 g, Total Carbohydrate 2.9 g, Dietary Fiber 1.2 g, Sugar 1.3 g

CABBAGE WRAPPED BRIE STUFFED MEATBALL

Prep Time 15 minutes
Cook Time 40 minutes
Total Time 55 minutes
Servings 2 - 3 slices

Ingredients

Meatball
- 4 oz (115 g) Cabbage Leaves (About 5 Big Leaves)
- 12 oz (340 g) Ground Pork
- 1/2 tsp Salt
- 1/4 tsp Black Pepper
- 1 tsp Dried Parsley
- 1/2 tsp Garlic Powder
- 1 tbsp Grated Parmesan Cheese
- 1 tbsp Worcestershire Sauce
- 1 wheel (4.5 oz / 125 g) Brie or Camembert Cheese

Sauce
- 1.5 tbsp Sugar Free Ketchup
- 2 tbsp Worcestershire Sauce
- 1 tsp Gluten Free Soy Sauce (or Coconut Aminos)

Topping
- 1/2 tsp Dried Parsley (or 1 tsp Fresh Chopped Parsley)

Instructions

1. Fill a pot with water and bring it to a boil. Parboil the cabbage leaves for 3 - 5 minutes with a lid on. Drain and pat the leaves dry with a towel. Set aside.
2. Preheat the oven to 200 C / 400 F.
3. In a mixing bowl, combine the ground pork, salt, pepper, parsley, garlic powder, parmesan and Worcestershire sauce. Knead the mixture until uniform.
4. Line an oven safe glass bowl with the cabbage leaves. (* A 6-inch / 15 cm bowl is used in the pictures.)

5. Add about 1/2 of the pork mixture to the bowl. Place the brie in the center and cover with the remaining 1/2 of the pork mixture.

6. Fold the ends of the cabbage leaves over the pork mixture.

7. Cover with aluminum foil and bake for 30 - 35 minutes.
8. [Sauce] Mix well the ketchup, Worcestershire sauce and soy sauce in a small bowl. Heat in a pan or microwave if desired. (* You can add the juice / grease from the baked meatball to the sauce.)
9. Remove the cabbage wrapped meatball from the oven. Let stand for 5 minutes. Then, carefully invert on a serving platter. (* Before inverting, make sure to remove the juice / grease from the baked meatball from the bowl. Add it to the sauce or discard.)
10. Pour the sauce on top and sprinkle the parsley.

Recipe Notes:
Adding 1 to 2 tbsp of heavy cream to the sauce is also recommended.

Approximate Nutritional Values Per Serving:
- 1/2:
  Calories 635 kcal, Protein 47.8 g, Total Fat 44.1 g, Total Carbohydrate 7.4 g, Dietary Fiber 1.0 g, Sugar 5.3 g
- 1/3:
  Calories 423 kcal, Protein 31.9 g, Total Fat 29.4 g, Total Carbohydrate 4.9 g, Dietary Fiber 0.7 g, Sugar 3.5 g

EGGS IN PORK BURGERS

Prep Time 10 minutes
Cook Time 23 minutes
Total Time 33 minutes
Servings 4

Ingredients
- 1 pound (450 g) Ground Pork
- 1 tbsp Worcestershire Sauce
- 2 tbsp Parmesan Cheese Powder
- 1 tsp Salt
- 1/2 tsp Black Pepper
- 1/4 cup (2 oz / 56 g) Shredded Mozzarella Cheese
- 4 Small to Medium Eggs

Toppings
- 1/4 cup (2 oz / 56 g) Shredded Mozzarella Cheese
- 1/4 tsp Black Pepper

Instructions
1. Preheat the oven to 200 C / 400 F.
2. In a bowl, combine the ground pork, Worcestershire sauce, parmesan, salt and black pepper. Knead the mixture until uniform.
3. Divide the mixture into 4 equal portions.
4. With each of the portions, form a ring (approx. sizes for ring: 4 inch / 10 cm and for hole: 2 inch / 5 cm) on a cooking sheet (lined with parchment paper).
5. Place the mozzarella in each hole.
6. Crack an egg in each hole over the mozzarella.
7. Sprinkle the topping mozzarella over each ring and the black pepper on each egg.
8. Bake for 20 - 23 minutes.

Recipe Notes:
If you like runny eggs, simply bake your pork rings without eggs for about 10 - 13 minutes, take them out from the oven, put cheese and eggs in holes, sprinkle cheese and black pepper on top and bake another 8 - 10 minutes.

You may have a little egg white overflow if the holes are not big enough or if your eggs are a bit large, which can end up okay after baking, because those crispy whites on the cooking sheet taste good anyway.

Approximate Nutritional Values Per Serving:
Calories 441 kcal, Protein 38.1 g, Total Fat 29.1 g, Total Carbohydrate 2.2 g, Dietary Fiber 0 g, Sugar 1.7 g

Creative Keto Kitchen

JAPANESE RAMEN

Prep Time 3 minutes
Cook Time 5 minutes
Total Time 8 minutes
Servings 1

Ingredients

Noodles
- 1 pack (7 oz / 200 g) Shirataki Noodles
- 2 tsp Salt (For Rubbing)
- 2 cups (240 cc) Water

Soup
- 2 cups (240 cc) Homemade Pork Broth (or Chicken Broth, but Pork Broth cooked with garlic, ginger, and salt and pepper at least is recommended)
- 1/2 tsp Salt
- A dash (or more) of Pepper
- 2 to 3 tsp Gluten Free Soy Sauce (or Coconut Aminos) (Adjust to your liking)
- 1 tsp Sesame Oil

Toppings
- Soft Boiled Egg, Pork Belly, Green Onions, Roasted Garlic, Nori Seaweed, etc

Instructions

To Remove Unpleasant Odor of Noodles
1. Drain the shirataki noodles.
2. Place the noodles in a resealable bag and add the salt for rubbing. Seal the bag.
3. Rub the salt over the noodles for 20 - 30 seconds.
4. Add the water to a saucepan. Add the noodles. Then turn the heat to high and bring to a boil.
5. Once boiled, remove from the heat (no need to cook longer) and drain the noodles. (* If your shirataki noodles are too long, just cut them with a kitchen knife or kitchen scissors here.)

Soup
1. Add the pork broth to a saucepan. Bring to a boil over high. Then reduce the heat to low.
2. Add the salt, pepper, soy sauce (or coconut aminos) and sesame oil.

Assembly
1. Add the shirataki noodles to the saucepan of soup and simmer over low heat for a minute. Remove from the heat.
2. Serve the noodles into a bowl and add the soup.
3. Top with your favorite toppings you've prepared.

Approximate Nutritional Values Per Serving:
No nutrition values for this recipe

CHICKEN OKRA TOMATO SOUP

Prep Time 5 minutes
Cook Time 20 minutes
Total Time 25 minutes
Servings 4

Ingredients

- 1.3 lbs (600 g) Chicken Thigh with Skin, Chopped
- 1 tbsp Butter
- 2 Tomatoes, Diced (About 11 oz / 300 g)
- 1 cup (240 cc) Chicken Broth
- 1 tbsp Grated Ginger
- 1 tsp Salt
- 1/2 tsp Black Pepper
- 1/2 tsp Dried Thyme
- 1/2 tsp Dried Basil
- 1/2 tsp Dried Oregano
- 2 tbsp Worcestershire Sauce
- 7 oz (200 g) Okra
- 4 tbsp Grated Parmesan Cheese

Instructions

To Cook in the Instant Pot

1. Press the 'Sauté' button on your Instant Pot to preheat. When hot, add the butter. Then add the chicken pieces and cook until brown.
2. Add the tomatoes and stir.
3. Add the chicken broth, ginger, salt, black pepper, thyme, basil, oregano, Worcestershire sauce and mix.
4. Close and lock the lid of the Instant Pot. Turn the pressure valve to 'SEAL'. Press the 'Pressure Cook' or 'Manual' button and adjust the timer to 8 minutes.
5. While pressure cooking, rinse the okra. Remove skin around top with calyx. Trim off the tip of the stem. Cut into 1-inch / 2.5 cm slices.
6. When the pressure cooking is done, release the pressure by using 'Quick Release' (= moving the pressure valve to venting position). Remove the Instant Pot lid.
7. Press the 'Sauté' button. Add the okra and simmer for 3 - 10 minutes, depending on how tender you want your okra to be.
8. Divide the soup among serving bowls. Sprinkle with the parmesan cheese.

To Cook on the Stove

1. In a pot over medium heat, add the butter. Then add the chicken and cook until brown.
2. Add the tomatoes and stir.
3. Add the chicken broth, ginger, salt, black pepper, thyme, basil, oregano, Worcestershire sauce and mix.
4. Simmer with the lid on over low heat for about 15 minutes.
5. While simmering, rinse the okra. Remove skin around top with calyx. Trim off the tip of the stem. Cut into 1-inch / 2.5 cm slices.
6. Open the lid and add the okra.
7. Simmer without the lid for 3 - 10 minutes over medium heat, depending on how tender you want your okra to be.
8. Divide the soup among serving bowls. Sprinkle with the parmesan cheese.

Recipe Notes:

If you want your okra to be really tender and soup to be thick, you can pressure cook (Instant Pot) or simmer with the lid on (Stove) at the same time as the chicken pieces.
The soup tastes better the next day.

Approximate Nutritional Values Per Serving:
Calories 443 kcal, Protein 33.3 g, Total Fat 29.4 g, Total Carbohydrate 9.3 g, Dietary Fiber 3.3 g, Sugar 5.5 g

JAPANESE CHICKEN CURRY

Cook Time 13 minutes
Total Time 13 minutes
Servings 4

Ingredients

- 1 tbsp Butter
- 2 cloves Garlic, Minced
- 1.3 lbs (600 g) Chicken Thigh with Skin, Chopped
- 1/2 tsp Salt
- 3/4 cup (180 cc) Chicken Broth
- 1/2 cup (120 cc) Tomato Puree
- 2 tbsp Curry Powder (Preferably Simply Organic's Curry Powder)
- 1/2 tsp Garam Masala
- 1/2 tsp All Spice
- 1 tsp Onion Powder
- 2 tbsp Worcestershire Sauce
- 1 tsp Gluten Free Soy Sauce (or Coconut Aminos)
- 1/2 tsp Xanthan Gum

Instructions

To Cook in the Instant Pot

1. Press the 'Sauté' button on your Instant Pot to preheat. When hot, add the butter. Then add the garlic.
2. Add the chicken pieces and cook until brown.
3. Add the salt.
4. Add the chicken broth and tomato puree and stir.
5. Add the curry powder, garam masala, all spice, onion powder, Worcestershire sauce and soy sauce and stir well. (* Add your favorite low carb vegetables here if you don't mind soft veges.)
6. Close and lock the lid of the Instant Pot. Close the pressure valve. Press the 'Pressure Cook' button and adjust cooking time to 8 minutes.
7. When the pressure cooking is done, open the pressure cooker by using 'Quick Release' (= moving the pressure valve to venting position).

8. Add the xanthan gum and stir with a whisk vigorously.
9. Serve with cauliflower rice.

To Cook on the Stove
1. In a pot over medium heat, add the butter. Then add the garlic.
2. Add the chicken and cook until brown.
3. Add the salt.
4. Add the chicken broth and tomato puree and stir.
5. Add the curry powder, garam masala, all spice, onion powder, Worcestershire sauce and soy sauce and stir well.
6. Simmer with the lid on but slightly ajar over low heat for about 15 minutes.
7. Open the lid. (* If the amount of soup is greatly reduced, add some more chicken broth or water.) Add the xanthan gum and stir with a whisk vigorously.
8. Serve with cauliflower rice.

Recipe Notes:
The curry will get much tastier the next day. Japanese curry is usually thickened with wheat flour, so xanthan gum is used as a thickener in this recipe.

The curry shown here is topped with steamed broccoli, but you can add your favorite low carb vegetables. Spinach is a good option. If you don't mind soft broccoli (or any other low carb veges), you can add before closing the lid of your Instant Pot.

Also, the curry shown here is topped with a hard boiled egg cut in half. A sunny side egg is also one of the most popular toppings.

Approximate Nutritional Values Per Serving:
Calories 370 kcal, Protein 26.1 g, Total Fat 25.0 g, Total Carbohydrate 7.7 g, Dietary Fiber 1.8 g, Sugar 5.4 g

BACON & NAPA CABBAGE HOT POT WITH BRIE

Prep Time 15 minutes
Cook Time 15 minutes
Total Time 30 minutes
Servings 4

Ingredients
- 8 Napa Cabbage Leaves (About 12 oz / 340 g)
- 12 slices Bacon
- 1 wheel (4.5 oz / 125 g) Brie
- 3 cups (720 cc) Vegetable Broth
- 1 tsp Garlic Powder (or 1 clove Fresh Garlic, Grated)
- 1/2 tsp Black Pepper

Instructions
1. Wash the napa cabbage leaves. Drain well.
2. Lay one napa cabbage leaf on a cutting board and then 2 slices of bacon on it. Repeat until you have four 4 layers of napa cabbage leaves.

3. Cut the napa cabbage leaves into 4 - 5 pieces to fit into your pot. (* The pot used in the picture -> Diameter: 8 inch / 20 cm x Height: 4 inch / 10 cm)

4. Pack the layered bacon and napa cabbage in the pot tightly, cross section up, creating a whirlpool pattern.

5. Put the brie cheese in the center. Score the top in a criss-cross with a knife if desired.
6. Add the vegetable stock. Sprinkle the garlic powder and black pepper.
7. Cook over medium heat with the lid on for 10 - 15 mins, until the napa cabbage is tender.

Recipe Notes:
This recipe is best for 8-inch / 20cm (diameter) x 4-inch / 10 cm (height) pots. Adjust the ingredients according to the size of your pot.
It tastes much better the next day, so cook beforehand, refrigerate, and reheat before serving.
American bacon may be cut thicker than Japanese bacon, so if you think it's too much bacon, reduce the amount.

Approximate Nutritional Values Per Serving:
Calories 355 kcal, Protein 14.5 g, Total Fat 31.3 g, Total Carbohydrate 3.9 g, Dietary Fiber 1.1 g, Sugar 2.7 g

SUSHI DONUTS

Prep Time 10 minutes
Cook Time 5 minutes
Total Time 15 minutes
+ Chilling Time
Servings 6 sushi donuts

Ingredients

Sushi Rice
- 10 oz (280 g) Frozen Riced Cauliflower
- 2 oz (56 g) Cream Cheese, Softened
- 2 tsp Apple Cider Vinegar
- 5 to 8 drops Liquid Stevia

Toppings
- 1/2 Cucumber (About 3 inch / 7.5 cm long)
- 12 slices Smoked Salmon (or Sashimi Grade Salmon)
- 1/2 Avocado
- 6 4-inch (10 cm) Square Nori Seaweed Sheets

To Garnish (Optional)
- Toasted Sesame Seeds, Egg Strips, Sprouts (such as Alfalfa), Mayo, etc

To Serve
- Gluten Free Soy Sauce or Coconut Aminos

Instructions

1. Cook the riced cauliflower in a frying pan for 3 - 5 minutes. Let cool.
2. In a large bowl, combine well the cauliflower rice, cream cheese, apple cider vinegar, and liquid stevia. Rest in the fridge for 15 - 20 minutes while preparing the veges.
3. [Cucumber] Using a vegetable peeler, thinly slice the cucumber lengthwise. Let stand on a kitchen paper for 5 minutes.
4. [Avocado] Slice the avocado lengthwise and cut each slice into half.
5. Arrange nicely the cucumber, salmon, and avocado in each cavity of a silicone donut mold.

6. Spoon the cauliflower rice into each cavity. Compress with the back of the spoon or your fingers.

7. Fold the ends of the cucumber slices and salmon over the cauliflower rice.
8. Rest in the fridge for 30 minutes, until set.
9. Invert the donut mold onto a serving plate and remove the mold.
10. Optional: Garnish more if desired.
11. To serve, using a cake server or a knife, place your sushi donut onto the nori. Pour soy sauce or coconut aminos over your sushi donut if desired. Grab and bite, or use chopsticks.

Approximate Nutritional Values Per Serving:
Calories 121 kcal, Protein 10.6 g, Total Fat 7.3 g, Total Carbohydrate 4.0 g, Dietary Fiber 2.4 g, Sugar 1.7 g

Creative Keto Kitchen

CURRIED EGG & AVOCADO SALAD CHEESE CUPS

Prep Time 20 minutes
Cook Time 8 minutes
Total Time 28 minutes
Servings 15 cups

Ingredients

Cheese Cups
- 1 1/2 cup (4.2 oz / 120 g) Shredded Cheddar Cheese

Egg & Avocado Salad
- 1/3 cup (75 g) Mayonnaise
- 1 tbsp Curry Powder
- 1 tsp Whole Grain Dijon Mustard
- 1/2 tsp Garlic Powder
- 1/2 tsp Black Pepper
- 4 Hard Boiled Eggs, Chopped
- 2 Avocados, Cubed

Toppings (Optional)
- 3 tbsp Yogurt
- 1/4 tsp Paprika Powder

Instructions

Cheese Cups
1. Preheat the oven to 180 C / 350 F.
2. Spoon one tablespoon of the cheddar cheese 2 inches / 5 cm apart on a baking sheet lined with parchment paper.
3. Bake for 6 - 8 minutes.
4. After removing from the oven, allow to cool for a minute.
5. Press the cheese circles into each mini muffin pan cavity to form the shape of a cup.
6. Let them cool until firm.

Egg & Avocado Salad
1. Mix well the mayonnaise, curry powder, Dijon mustard, garlic powder and black pepper in a bowl.
2. Add the chopped hard boiled eggs and cubed avocados in a large bowl and add the curry sauce and stir well.

Assembly
1. Place about 2 tablespoons of the egg and avocado salad in each cheese cup.
2. Optional: Place the yogurt in a piping bag and pipe on top. Sprinkle the paprika on top.
3. Serve immediately.

Approximate Nutritional Values Per Serving
Sans Yogurt and Paprika**:**
Calories 135 kcal, Protein 4.6 g, Total Fat 12.2 g, Total Carbohydrate 2.3 g, Dietary Fiber 1.3 g, Sugar 1.0 g

Creative Keto Kitchen

CAULIFLOWER RICE ONIGIRAZU

Prep Time 15 minutes
Cook Time 10 minutes
Total Time 25 minutes
+ Chilling Time
Servings 4 onigirazu

Ingredients

Cauliflower Rice (For 4 Onigirazu)
- 10 oz (280 g) Frozen Riced Cauliflower
- 1 tbsp Unsalted Butter
- 1 clove Garlic, Minced
- 1/2 tsp Salt
- 1/2 tsp Black Pepper
- 1 oz (28 g) Cream Cheese

Chicken & Hard Boiled Egg (For 2 Onigirazu)
- 3.5 oz (100 g) Shredded Chicken
- 2 tbsp Mayonnaise
- 1 tsp Whole Grain Mustard
- 1/4 tsp Salt
- 1/8 tsp Black Pepper
- 2 leaves Lettuce
- 1/2 Avocado, Sliced into 4 Pieces
- 2 Hard Boiled Eggs
- 2 8-inch Square Nori Seaweed Sheets

Ham & Omelette (For 2 Onigirazu)
- 2 Eggs
- 1 tbsp Heavy Cream
- 1/4 tsp Salt
- 1/8 tsp Black Pepper
- 1 tbsp Avocado Oil
- 4 leaves Lettuce
- 4 slices Ham
- 1/2 Avocado, Sliced into 6 Pieces
- 2 tbsp Mayonnaise
- 2 8-inch Square Nori Seaweed Sheets

Instructions

Cauliflower Rice (For 4 Onigirazu)
1. In a frying pan over medium heat, melt the butter. Add the garlic.
2. Add the riced cauliflower and cook for 3 - 5 minutes. Add the salt and pepper and stir.
3. Turn off the heat, then add the cream cheese. Stir until combined.

Chicken & Hard Boiled Egg
1. In a bowl, mix well the shredded chicken, mayonnaise, mustard, salt and pepper.
2. Place a large piece of plastic wrap on a working surface and put a nori sheet on top with the shiny side facing down.
3. Spread the cooked cauliflower rice (1/8 of the total quantity) in a square shape in the center of the nori sheet, with the tip of the square at the top of the nori sheet.
4. Place one lettuce leaf on top of the cauliflower rice, then 2 avocado slices on top.

5. Place one hard boiled egg between the avocado slices.

6. Place 1/2 of the shredded chicken on top, then cauliflower rice on top of the chicken. (* It may get messy.)

7. Pull one corner of the nori sheet towards the center of the filling, then the opposite corner towards the center.

8. Then bring the other 2 corners towards the center of the filling and seal tightly with the plastic wrap.

9. Repeat with the rest of the ingredients to make one more onigirazu.
10. Rest 15 - 30 minutes in the fridge.
11. Slice in half with the plastic wrap still on.

Ham & Omelette
1. In a bowl, beat the eggs, heavy cream, salt and pepper until blended. Heat 1/2 of the avocado oil in a frying pan over medium heat until hot. Tilt the pan to coat the bottom, then pour in 1/2 of the egg mixture. Tilt the pan to distribute the egg mixture evenly. Leave for 20 - 30 seconds. Using a spatula or wooden spoon, bring the edges to the center to form into a square. Set aside. Repeat with the rest to make one more omelette.

2. Place a large piece of plastic wrap on a working surface and put a nori sheet on top with the shiny side facing down.
3. Spread the cooked cauliflower rice in a square shape in the center of the nori sheet, with the tip of the square at the top of the nori sheet.
4. Place one lettuce leaf on top of the cauliflower rice, then one slice of ham on top.
5. Spread 1/2 of the mayonnaise over the ham.
6. Place 3 avocado slices, one square omelette, then another slice of ham.

7. Place one lettuce leaf, then cauliflower rice on top.
8. Pull one corner of the nori sheet towards the center of the filling, then the opposite corner towards the center.
9. Then bring the other 2 corners towards the center and seal tightly with the plastic wrap.
10. Repeat with the rest of the ingredients to make one more onigirazu.
11. Rest 15 - 30 minutes in the fridge.
12. Slice in half with the plastic wrap still on.

Recipe Notes:
When meal prepping for the week, omit avocado, which will turn brown.

Approximate Nutritional Values Per Serving:
- One Whole Chicken & Hard Boiled Egg Onigirazu: Calories 364 kcal, Protein 21.2 g, Total Fat 27.8 g, Total Carbohydrate 7.2 g, Dietary Fiber 3.3 g, Sugar 3.8 g
- One Whole Ham & Omelette Onigirazu: Calories 387 kcal, Protein 16.5 g, Total Fat 32.8 g, Total Carbohydrate 7.3 g, Dietary Fiber 3.3 g, Sugar 4.0 g

SALMON & AVOCADO POCKETS

Prep Time 10 minutes
Total Time 10 minutes
Servings 10 pieces

Ingredients
- 2.5 oz (70 g) Cream Cheese
- 1/2 Avocado
- 1 tsp Lemon Juice
- 1 tbsp Mayonnaise
- A Pinch of Salt
- A Pinch of Black Pepper
- 20 slices Smoked Salmon (About 10.5 oz / 300 g)

Instructions
1. Add the cream cheese, avocado, lemon juice, mayo, salt and black pepper to a food processor. Blend well.
2. Place one slice of the smoked salmon vertically and one slice horizontally, making a cross. Place 1/10 of the avocado mixture in the middle. Close the salmon slices to make a bundle. Repeat with the remaining mixture.
3. Chill if desired.
4. Optional: Decorate Jack O' Lantern faces for Halloween if desired. (See the Recipe Notes below for ideas.)

Recipe Notes:
Decoration Ideas: Using nori seaweed is very popular in Japan when decorating faces on foods, such as on rice balls. It will be delicate work, which requires tweezers or chopsticks. Also, parsley stems can be used to resemble pumpkin stems.

Approximate Nutritional Values Per Serving:
Calories 89 kcal, Protein 8.4 g, Total Fat 5.6 g, Total Carbohydrate 0.5 g, Dietary Fiber 0.2 g, Sugar 0.3 g

BRAIDED CUCUMBER SUSHI

Prep Time 15 minutes
Cook Time 5 minutes
Total Time 20 minutes
+ Chilling Time
Servings 6 pieces

Ingredients

- 8.5 oz (240 g) Frozen Riced Cauliflower
- 2 oz (56 g) Cream Cheese, Softened
- 2 tsp Toasted Sesame Seeds
- 2 tsp Apple Cider Vinegar
- 5 to 8 drops Liquid Stevia
- 1 tsp Gluten Free Soy Sauce (or Coconut Aminos)
- 1 Cucumber (About 8 inch / 20 cm long)
- 6 slices Smoked Salmon (or Sashimi Grade Salmon)
- 1 Avocado

To Serve
- Gluten Free Soy Sauce (or Coconut Aminos)

Instructions

1. Cook the riced cauliflower in a frying pan for 3 - 5 minutes. Let cool.
2. In a large bowl, combine well the cauliflower, cream cheese, sesame, apple cider vinegar, soy sauce and liquid stevia. Rest in the fridge while preparing the cucumber, avocado, and salmon.
3. [Cucumber] Using a vegetable peeler, thinly slice the cucumber lengthwise. Pile up, then, cut in half lengthwise, then crosswise.

4. [Avocado] Cut the avocado in half. Remove the pit and skin. Slice lengthwise and cut each slice into half.
5. [Salmon] Cut each slice of the smoked salmon into half.
6. On a kitchen paper (to remove excess moisture), weave 7 strips of cucumber, 4 vertically and 3 horizontally. Place the weave into a cavity of a silicone muffin mold. Repeat until you get 6 weaves.

7. Fill 1/2 of each cavity of the muffin mold with 1/2 of the cauliflower rice. Compress with the back of a spoon or your fingers.
8. Place the salmon and avocado over the cauliflower rice.
9. Fill each cavity of the muffin mold with the remaining cauliflower rice. Compress with the back of the spoon or your fingers.

10. Rest in the fridge for 30 minutes, until set.
11. Invert the muffin mold onto a serving plate and carefully remove the mold.
12. Optional: Garnish as you like.
13. Pour soy sauce or coconut aminos over your sushi if desired.

Approximate Nutritional Values Per Serving:
Calories 125 kcal, Protein 6.9 g, Total Fat 9.3 g, Total Carbohydrate 4.7 g, Dietary Fiber 2.8 g, Sugar 1.9 g

JAPANESE OMELETTE (TAMAGOYAKI)

Prep Time 3 minutes
Cook Time 5 minutes
Total Time 8 minutes

Ingredients

Ham & Cheese
- 3 Eggs
- 1 tbsp Heavy Cream
- 1 tsp Soy Sauce (Optional)
- A Pinch of Salt
- A Pinch of Pepper
- 2 tsp Coconut Oil
- 2 slices Ham, Chopped
- 3 tbsp Shredded Mozzarella Cheese

Chives & Mayo
- 3 Eggs
- 1 tbsp Heavy Cream
- 1 tsp Soy Sauce (Optional)
- A Pinch of Salt
- A Pinch of Pepper
- 2 tsp Coconut Oil
- 2 tbsp Chives
- 3 tbsp Mayonnaise

Instructions

Ham & Cheese
1. Add the eggs, heavy cream, soy sauce, salt and pepper to a bowl and whisk well. Add the ham and mix.
2. Heat a tamagoyaki pan over medium. Once the pan gets hot, put one teaspoon of the coconut oil in the pan and tilt the pan to spread out on the pan.
3. Pour 1/3 of the egg mixture in the pan. Quickly distribute in the pan.
4. Place 1/2 of the shredded cheese.

5. When the bottom of the egg has set, start rolling it into a log using a spatula.

6. Push the rolled omelette to the other side, and repeat. (* Put some more coconut oil before pouring in the egg mixture.) Make sure to lift the omelette to distribute the mixture underneath.

7. Remove from the pan and slice.

Chives & Mayo
1. Add the eggs, heavy cream, soy sauce, salt and pepper to a bowl and whisk well. Add the chives and mix.
2. Heat a tamagoyaki pan over medium. Once the pan gets hot, put one teaspoon of the coconut oil in the pan and tilt the pan to spread out on the pan.
3. Pour 1/3 of the egg mixture in the pan. Quickly distribute in the pan.
4. Place 1/2 of the mayonnaise.
5. When the bottom of the egg has set, start rolling it into a log using a spatula.
6. Push the rolled omelette to the other side, and repeat. (* Put some more coconut oil before pouring in the egg mixture.) Make sure to lift the omelette to distribute the mixture underneath.
7. Remove from the pan and slice.

Recipe Notes:
You can find **Tamagoyaki Japanese Omelette Pans** on Amazon.

Approximate Nutritional Values Per Serving:
- One Whole Ham & Cheese Omelette:
  Calories 503 kcal, Protein 31.0 g, Total Fat 40.0 g, Total Carbohydrate 2.0 g, Dietary Fiber 0 g, Sugar 1.7 g
- One Whole Chives & Mayo Omelette:
  Calories 623 kcal, Protein 19.5 g, Total Fat 58.1 g, Total Carbohydrate 2.9 g, Dietary Fiber 0.3 g, Sugar 2.6 g

JAPANESE STYLE BLACK SESAME GREEN BEANS

Prep Time 5 minutes
Cook Time 3 minutes
Total Time 8 minutes
Servings 2

Ingredients

- 15 to 20 Green Beans (About 6 oz / 170 g)
- 3 cups (720 cc) Water
- 1 tsp Salt

Black Sesame Sauce

- 1 tbsp Roasted Black Sesame Seeds (or White Sesame Seeds), Ground
- 1 tbsp Gluten Free Soy Sauce (or Coconut Aminos)
- 2 to 3 drops Liquid Stevia

Instructions

1. Cut off both ends of the green beans.
2. Bring the water to a boil in a saucepan and add the salt.
3. Add the green beans to the saucepan and cook them for 2 - 3 minutes.
4. Drain the green beans and wash over with cold water. Then, wipe off excess water with some paper towels.
5. Cut the green beans into 2-inch / 5 cm pieces.
6. In a small bowl, combine all the sauce ingredients and mix well.
7. Pour the sauce over the green beans, toss, and serve.

Approximate Nutritional Values Per Serving:
Calories 41 kcal, Protein 2.8 g, Total Fat 1.7 g, Total Carbohydrate 4.7 g, Dietary Fiber 1.5 g, Sugar 3.2 g

BACON WRAPPED AVOCADO STUFFED BRIE

Prep Time 5 minutes
Cook Time 20 minutes
Total Time 25 minutes
Servings 4

Ingredients

- 1 wheel (4.5 oz / 125 g) Brie or Camembert Cheese
- 1/4 Avocado, Sliced into 3 Pieces
- 1 tbsp Mayonnaise
- 3 slices Bacon
- A Pinch of Black Pepper

Instructions

1. Preheat the oven to 200 C / 400 F.
2. Cut the brie in half so you have 2 round sections. Place the avocado slices on one of them and spread the mayo. Then, top with the other half of brie.
3. Lay the bacon slices on a cutting board in a radiating pattern and place the avocado stuffed brie in the center. Wrap the brie tightly with the bacon slices.

4. Invert and place on a cast iron skillet with the seam side down. Sprinkle the black pepper.
5. Bake for 20 minutes.

Recipe Notes:
This recipe was newly created for this cookbook.
Approximate Nutritional Values Per Serving:
Calories 192 kcal, Protein 8.1 g, Total Fat 17.2 g, Total Carbohydrate 0.9 g, Dietary Fiber 0.4 g, Sugar 0.5 g

HOMEMADE PROTEIN CHIPS

Prep Time 5 minutes
Cook Time 15 minutes
Total Time 20 minutes
Servings 4

Ingredients

- 5 tbsp (25 g) Whey Protein Powder
- 1 oz (28 g) Coconut Oil, Melted
- 2 tbsp Hot Water (See the Recipe Notes below)
- 1/2 to 1 tsp Salt (or Flavor of Choice such as Garlic Powder) (Adjust)

Instructions

1. Preheat the oven to 160 C / 320 F. Line a baking sheet with parchment paper.
2. In a medium bowl, combine the whey protein powder and melted coconut oil together.
3. Add the hot water and mix well.
4. Add the salt and mix well.
5. Place the mixture on the parchment paper and spread it as thin as possible (approximately into a 14 x 10 inch / 35 x 25 cm rectangle.)

6. Bake for about 15 minutes or until golden brown and crispy.
7. When cool enough to touch, break into pieces.

Recipe Notes:

Keep them in an air tight container / ziploc bag. Eat within 4 - 5 days.
They freeze well.
The consistency of the mixture may depend on the whey protein powder you use, so if you find the texture of your batter too thick or too thin before placing it on the parchment paper, adjust it by simply adding more coconut oil / water if thick or more protein powder if thin. The mixture should be creamy but a bit runny so that it is easy to spread it on the parchment paper as thin as possible (thin enough to be able to see the parchment paper through the mixture). Otherwise the texture will be dry and crumbly on the palate. The thinner, the crispier. Spreading the mixture as thin as possible before baking is the key to success. Also, bake well until crispy. Find what the optimal baking time is for your oven.

Because whey protein powder has a tendency to not dissolve well in very hot liquid, both coconut oil and water are hot, the protein powder may not dissolve completely and get lumpy. So, if you melt your coconut oil because it was solid, make sure that the oil is not very hot when adding. If it is, let it cool a bit OR add tepid water (instead of the hot water that is called for).

Approximate Nutritional Values Per Serving:
Calories 85 kcal, Protein 4.5 g, Total Fat 7.5 g, Total Carbohydrate 0.5 g, Dietary Fiber 0 g, Sugar 0 g

CINNAMON PROTEIN CHIPS

Prep Time 5 minutes
Cook Time 17 minutes
Total Time 22 minutes
Servings 4

Ingredients

Protein Chips
- 1 oz (28 g) Melted Unsalted Butter, Room Temp
- 2 tbsp Water
- 1 tsp Vanilla Extract
- 5 tbsp (25 g) Whey Protein Powder
- A Pinch of Stevia Powder
- 1 tsp Ground Cinnamon

Cinnamon Sweetener Mixture
- 2 tsp Granular Swerve
- 1/2 tsp Ground Cinnamon
- A Pinch of Stevia Powder

Cream Cheese Dip
- 4 oz (112 g) Cream Cheese
- 1/3 cup (80 cc) Heavy Cream
- 1 tsp Stevia Powder
- 1 tsp Vanilla Extract

Instructions

1. Preheat the oven to 160 C / 320 F. Line a baking sheet with parchment paper.
2. In a bowl, combine together the butter, water and vanilla.
3. Add the whey protein powder and mix until combined.
4. Add the stevia and cinnamon and mix until combined.
5. Place the batter on the parchment paper and spread it as thin as possible

(approximately into a 14 x 10 inch / 35 x 25 cm/ rectangle.)
6. Bake for 10 minutes.
7. While baking, combine the Swerve, cinnamon and stevia in a small bowl. Remove the baking sheet from the oven. (* Do not turn off the oven yet.) Sprinkle the cinnamon sweetener mixture. (* If you couldn't spread your batter large enough to the size mentioned above (14 x 10 inch / 35 x 25 cm), sprinkle less of the cinnamon sweetener mix than the quantity called for in the recipe because the baked chips may not get crispy.)

8. Bake for another 5 - 7 minutes. (* Watch closely 4 - 5 minutes after transferring back to the oven. The surface easily gets burnt.)
9. Let cool on the baking sheet. (* It may be soft when hot but will get hard as it cools.)
10. When cool enough to touch, break into pieces.

by simply adding more melted butter if thick or more protein powder if thin. The mixture should be creamy but a bit runny so that it is easy to spread it on the parchment paper as thin as possible (thin enough to be able to see the parchment paper through the mixture). The thinner, the crispier. Find what the optimal baking time is for your oven. Because whey protein powder has a tendency to not dissolve well in very hot liquid, make sure that the melted butter is not hot.

Approximate Nutritional Values Per Serving:
- **Without** Cream Cheese Dip:
  Calories 77 kcal, Protein 4.5 g, Total Fat 6.3 g, Total Carbohydrate 0.9 g, Dietary Fiber 0.3 g, Sugar 0.2 g
- **With** Cream Cheese Dip:
  Calories 263 kcal, Protein 7.3 g, Total Fat 24.8 g, Total Carbohydrate 2.2 g, Dietary Fiber 0.3 g, Sugar 1.5 g
  (Swerve is not counted as carbs as it doesn't affect blood sugar levels.)

Cream Cheese Dip
1. Combine all the ingredients together in a food processor.

Recipe Notes:
Keep them in an air tight container / ziploc bag. Eat within 4 - 5 days.
They freeze well.
The consistency of the mixture may depend on the whey protein powder you use, so if you find the texture of the protein mixture too thick or too thin before placing it on the parchment paper, adjust it

HOMEMADE "DORITOS"

Prep Time 5 minutes
Cook Time 18 minutes
Total Time 23 minutes
Servings 4

Ingredients
- 0.75 oz (21 g) Avocado Oil (Can sub melted unsalted butter, room temp)
- 3 tbsp Water
- 0.7 oz (20 g) Whey Protein Isolate (About 4 tbsp)
- 0.88 oz (25 g) Finely Grated Parmesan Cheese (Powdery) (About 1/4 cup)
- 1 oz (28 g) Grated Red Cheddar
- 1 tsp Garlic Powder
- 1 tsp Chili Powder
- 1/2 tsp Onion Powder
- 1/2 tsp Cumin
- 1/2 tsp Smoked Paprika
- 1/2 tsp Sea Salt

Instructions
1. Preheat the oven to 160 C / 320 F. Line a baking sheet with parchment paper.
2. In a bowl, combine together the avocado oil, water and whey protein isolate.
3. While letting the whey protein mixture sit for a couple minutes, in another bowl, mix well the garlic powder, chili powder, onion powder, cumin, smoked paprika, and sea salt. Divide into 2 equal portions (2 teaspoons each). Reserve one portion.
4. Add the other portion of the seasoning mixture and finely grated parmesan to the whey protein mixture. Stir until well combined.
5. Place the mixture on the parchment paper and spread it as thin as possible.

6. Sprinkle the red cheddar cheese.

7. Bake for 3 minutes.
8. Remove from the oven. Sprinkle the reserved seasoning. (Adjust if you don't like the flavor to be strong.)

9. Bake for another 15 minutes, or until crispy.
10. Let cool for 10 minutes, then break into pieces.

Recipe Notes:
Keep them in an air tight container / ziploc bag.
Approximate Nutritional Values Per Serving:
Calories 123 kcal, Protein 8.1 g, Total Fat 9.9 g, Total Carbohydrate 0.6 g, Dietary Fiber 0 g, Sugar 0.4 g

Recipe Index

VANILLA CUSTARD BLUEBERRY MUFFINS 4

CREAMY LEMON CURD RASPBERRY MUFFINS 6

TWO-TONE CINNAMON DONUTS 8

COCONUT COOKIES 10

CINNAMON CHOCOLATE COCONUT FLOUR COOKIES 11

LEMON CREAM CHEESE COOKIES 12

LINGOTS AU CHOCOLAT 14

ALMOND BUTTER BROWNIES 17

CARAMEL SWIRL POUND CAKE 18

CHOCOLATE & CARAMEL MOUSSE CAKE WITH COFFEE CARAMEL GLAZE 20

TIRAMISU 23

NO-BAKE PEANUT BUTTER CHOCOLATE ZEBRA CHEESECAKE 26

COCONUT FLOUR VANILLA LAYER CAKE WITH BLUEBERRY FILLING 28

THREE LAYER RASPBERRY CHEESECAKE MOUSSE TERRINE 30

TRICOLOUR BUNDT CAKE (VANILLA, CHOCOLATE & CINNAMON) 32

CARAMEL CHEESECAKE BARS 34

ZEBRA CAKE 36

CHOCOLATE TERRINE 38

NO-BAKE CHEESECAKE WITH LEMON CURD FILLING 40

CINNAMON BUNDT CAKE 42

CHOCOLATE CHIP BROWNIE TOWER 44

NO CRUST BAKED CHEESECAKE WITH BLUEBERRY COMPOTE 46

CHOCOLATE ÉCLAIR CUPS WITH CARAMEL SAUCE 68

DOUBLE CHOCOLATE LAYER CAKE 48

NO-CHURN AVOCADO STRAWBERRY PROTEIN ICE CREAM 71

RASPBERRY JELLY DOUBLE CHOCOLATE CHEESECAKE 50

CHOCOLATE DIPPED ICE CREAM TACOS (HOMEMADE CHOCO TACO) 72

FLOURLESS PEANUT BUTTER CHOCOLATE CAKE 52

AVOCADO BERRY COCONUT CREAM POPSICLES 75

LEMON JELLO CHEESECAKE 54

NO-CHURN PEANUT BUTTER ICE CREAM 76

CHOCOLATE BUTTERCREAM MERINGUE TOWER CAKE 56

TIRAMISU POPSICLES 78

SOUFFLE CUSTARD PIE 58

FROZEN PUMPKIN BITES 80

ALMOND BUTTER CHOCOLATE PIE 60

MERINGUE COOKIE PEANUT BUTTER CHOCOLATE BARS 82

VANILLA CUSTARD CHOCOLATE TARTLETS 62

MELT-IN-YOUR-MOUTH CHOCOLATE FUDGE 84

BUTTERY ALMOND TARTLETS 64

COFFEE JELLY 85

PEANUT BUTTER CHOCOLATE MOUSSE TART 66

STRAWBERRY & YOGURT MOUSSE 86

STRAWBERRY-STUFFED NO-BAKE CHOCOLATE CHEESECAKE BITES 88

CHOCOLATE BABKA 106

PEANUT BUTTER MASCARPONE JARS 90

CINNAMON BABKA WITH CINNAMON GLAZE 108

PANNA COTTA WITH BERRY JELLY 92

FRENCH SAVORY CAKE (CAKE SALE) 111

MAGIC COFFEE MOUSSE 94

HAM, CREAM CHEESE & NUTS PULL-APART RING 112

MAPLE NUT BRIE 96

CHOCOLATE CINNAMON PULL-APART BREAD 114

LEMON CHEESECAKE SMOOTHIE 97

PEANUT BUTTER STUFFED SKILLET ROLLS WITH CHOCOLATE DIPPING SAUCE 116

AVOCADO CHOCOLATE SMOOTHIE 98

CHEESEBURGER STUFFED BAGUETTE 118

SUPER-EASY KETO BREAD 99

HAM & EGG BUNS 120

CREAM CHEESE DANISH 100

GARLIC SHRIMP AVOCADO BREAD 122

CHEESY COCONUT FLOUR BISCUITS 103

BERRY TWIST BUNS 124

CURRY PUFFS 104

SALMON AVOCADO CROQUE CAKE 126

ZUCCHINI & HAM PASTRY ROSES 128

CHEESY AVOCADO STUFFED CHICKEN BURGERS 148

CHOCOLATE CREAM HORNS 130

DAIKON RADISH POTSTICKERS (JAPANESE GYOZA) 150

BACON PAIN d'EPI 132

BACON WRAPPED BROCCOLI STUFFED PORK CHOPS 152

CHEESY WEAVE 134

CABBAGE WRAPPED BRIE STUFFED MEATBALL 154

SOUFFLE QUICHE 136

EGGS IN PORK BURGERS 156

BACON & CHEESE WRAPPED PORK BELLY 138

JAPANESE RAMEN 158

CURRIED EGG ZUCCHINI BOATS 140

CHICKEN OKRA TOMATO SOUP 160

PORK BURGER WRAPPED OKRA 141

JAPANESE CHICKEN CURRY 162

EGG, BACON & CHEESE STUFFED MEATLOAF 142

BACON & NAPA CABBAGE HOT POT WITH BRIE 164

CHICKEN CRUST HAM & BROCCOLI PIE 144

SUSHI DONUTS 166

PAN-FRIED BACON WRAPPED ZUCCHINI SKEWERS 146

CURRIED EGG & AVOCADO SALAD CHEESE CUPS 168

Creative Keto Kitchen

CAULIFLOWER RICE ONIGIRAZU 170

SALMON & AVOCADO POCKETS 173

BRAIDED CUCUMBER SUSHI 174

JAPANESE OMELETTE (TAMAGOYAKI) 176

JAPANESE STYLE BLACK SESAME GREEN BEANS 178

BACON WRAPPED AVOCADO STUFFED BRIE 179

HOMEMADE PROTEIN CHIPS 180

CINNAMON PROTEIN CHIPS 182

HOMEMADE "DORITOS" 184

Made in the USA
Columbia, SC
15 August 2019